A Legacy to Remember: "Recollections Of a Common Man"

A Legacy to Remember: "Recollections Of a Common Man"

A Biography of Duard Vinson Gillum

Edited by:
Pamela K. Orgeron, M.A., Ed.S., BCCC, ACLC

ABC's Ministries
Nashville, TN 37115

A Legacy to Remember: "Recollections of a Common Man"
Copyright © 2018 by ABC's Ministries. All rights reserved.

Library of Congress Control Number: Pending
ISBN PB 978-0-9979565-5-9

Printed in the United States of America

No part of this publication may be reproduced or transmitted in any form or by any means without written permission of the editor or publisher.

Dedication

I dedicate this book in memory of Duard Vinson Gillum "Tiny", whose life this book documents. A cousin, dear friend, and brother in Christ, "Tiny" impacted my life in many ways. He was such an encourager to me. No doubt he touched the lives of his other relatives, to whom I also dedicate this book.

Contents

Forward	xi
Preface	xii
1. The Depression: Born into Poverty	1
2. The School Years	20
3. World War II…Stateside	38
4. World War II…Sea Duty	64
5. The Attitude Adjustment Years	100
6. California…The 1st Dozen Years	117
7. California…The 2nd Dozen Years	140
8. A Prelude to Retirement	155
9. The Retirement Years	173
10. The Waning Years	211
11. Just Like an Uncle	221
(Written by Cousin Pamela K. Orgeron)	
Appendix: A Tribute to Mam-Maw Keaton	237
About the Editor	244

Foreword*

Many stories have been written about famous people. The lives and accomplishments of Presidents, Kings, War Heroes, Authors and Sports Figures have been detailed in biographies and best-selling novels throughout history. The story of my life is far removed from that category, and is not remotely intended to suggest otherwise.

The real-life character depicted here is not, has never been, and is not expected to be famous.

These words were written to satisfy a personal desire to recall and record the many memories; some good, and some not good. They are the memories of an ordinary Kentucky lad born prior to (but who experienced the brunt of) the Great Depression years (1929-1934). The accounts are factual, and written from personal memory with invaluable contributions from my brother, Cliff, whose recall is so much better than that of my own.

There is no intent to imply that life has been unfair, nor is any praise or pity solicited. Without doubt, similar stories could be written by many others who lived during this era.

D. V. Gillum

*Excerpted from *Recollections of a Common Man* (Xlibris, 2011)

Preface

When I wrote my first book *The ABC's of Life for Children and Adults: Short Stories, Essays, and Poems Promoting Christian Concepts* (Xulon Press, 2003), little did I realize that we already had an author in the family, my father's first cousin Duard Vinson Gillum, better known to me as "Tiny". Whenever Tiny was visiting us in Kentucky in 2003 he read my first book pre-publication. At that time he told me that he too had written a book about his life story. Immediately I asked him for a copy. I told him if he gave me a copy of his book, I would send him a copy of mine once published. He said, "Yes, we can do that." Whenever Tiny formally published his autobiography in 2011 shortly before his death, he was true to his word and mailed me a copy of his book.

Before I read Tiny's autobiography, *Recollections of a Common Man* (Xlibris, 2011) I knew little about my father's roots. Knowing how close Tiny and Dad were as children, well, actually their entire lives, I couldn't wait to learn more about my roots. One thought I had after reading Tiny's tribute about my great grandmother Mam-Maw Keaton (aka, Mam-Maw Smith) was that I'm glad he had such positive feelings for her; because honestly, I would not have liked her, or at least, I wouldn't have appreciated her use of tobacco. Don't think I wouldn't have told her either!!!

After reading *Recollections of a Common Man* my love and respect for Tiny, who shared my love of the Lord, grew by leaps and bounds. He was so humble. He also enjoyed life in spite of having experienced so much tragedy in his life—the Great Depression, living in poverty, World War II and the death of a child, which triggered a divorce. Many people would have been bitter having lived through all that; but, not Tiny. He was always very kind to everyone. Everyone loved him.

Knowing how hard of a time I was having promoting my own book and getting book sales, I wanted to help Tiny in promoting his book. I started loaning my copy of *Recollections of a Common Man* (Xlibris, 2011) to personal friends whom I thought might like the book. The most common response was, "I liked the book; but, I was distracted by all the typos and grammatical errors."

With the responses from my friends about Tiny's book, I thought, *I could edit the book for him*. However, not until now has God cleared my scheduled and led me to begin work on this new book project. Some may wonder why I am doing this now that a few years back Tiny moved on to receive his Heavenly reward.

First, I am doing this to honor Tiny and knowing how much he wanted his descendants to benefit from reading his life story. Additionally, Tiny had a desire for one or more of his descendants to write the last chapter of his book. In *Recollections of a Common Man* (Xlibris, 2011), he wrote in the book's conclusion,

> This book, in addition to being a chronicle of my life and times, is left to those who will succeed me, whether they be family or friends, or both. To them, I entrust the final chapter, hoping that someday, someone will take what is thus far advanced and carry it forward . . . that he, she, or they will chronicle events subsequent to these and of their lives and times . . . and in so doing, continue this as a book of Family Heritage. (p. 211)

When chatting with a mutual cousin of Tiny's and mine a few days ago, she did not even know he had written a book. That was one of the other factors that gave me the incentive to start this new book project, which I have entitled,

A Legacy to Remember: "Recollections of a Common Man", to bring more visibility to Tiny's story and his autobiography.

Through sharing Tiny's life story I hope not only descendants of Tiny's; but my own descendants will benefit from the lessons shared in the book. I also believe that others in the general public will find value in reading about the life story and testimony of Tiny.

Pamela K. Orgeron
August 1, 2018

CHAPTER 1

The Depression: Born into Poverty

In the 1920's, Eastern Kentucky's Floyd County residents depended mainly on coal mining as their principal source of employment. If a man was not a coal miner, he was a farmer. More often he was forced to be both just to make ends meet. Rearing a family on nothing more than a miner's pay was difficult. Many small communities were built by the mine owners to provide their workers the essentials necessary for rearing a family. Each community had doctors and hospitals to serve the local needs. In addition to the medical services and facilities, housing, schools, churches, and stores were included in the town layout. One such town was Wayland, Kentucky, a small community nestled along the banks of Right Beaver Creek.

July 28, 1925 the editor of this book's cousin "Tiny" was born in Wayland, Kentucky to Andrew Jackson and Ida May Gillum. He joined his two older brothers Clifford Frank, then 3.5 years old, and Buford Clayton (nickname: Bootie), then 22 months of age.

Christened Duard Vinson, Tiny never knew how his mother came up with his name. Tiny's paternal grandparents, Henry Gilliam and Betsy Jane Lemaster Gilliam were not living when he was born. However, he was blessed to know his maternal grandparents, Augustus Smith and Mary Melissa Keaton Smith.

Although being named Duard Vinson was bad enough, there was more to come! Cliff had a playmate named Claude. Cliff's youngest brother was merely a "tiny Claude" to him, Thus, Cliff gave Tiny his first nickname.

"THE GILLUM THREE"
left to right
Buford Clayton, Duard Vinson, Clifford Frank
in their innocent stages

After moving to California as an adult, "Tiny" acquired a new nickname, "Gill". To his family and friends in California, he was known as Gill, but to some of his relatives and friends in the East who grew up with him, he still carries the nickname "Tiny". On a side note, Tiny's cousin, Pam Orgeron, the editor of *A Legacy to Remember*, remembers when Tiny was visiting her family and he told her father that he was then using the nickname "Gill". When Pam's father told Tiny, "I have known you so long as 'Tiny', I don't know whether I can remember to do that."

"That's okay. I understand," Tiny replied. He was always understanding and flexible like that.

Located across the swinging foot bridge spanning Beaver Creek was a somewhat smaller community named Glo. Tiny's parents and brothers lived in Glo before his birth. Tiny's father, Mr. Gilliam, first worked in the mines as an ordinary miner, but as work became more plentiful, he hired a crew on his own, and thereafter subcontracted his services to the mine owners. This provided a substantially larger income, and enabled the Gilliam family to move to Wayland, and larger living quarters.

Coal mining is a very dangerous occupation, and major accidents were not uncommon. Mr. Gilliam was involved in at least two cave-ins that resulted in broken bones. Miners were paid twice a month, thus each payday was known as a "half". Rarely, if ever, did money from one "half" last to the next. That, in turn, gave rise to the "company store" where all essentials were purchased. The company store's policy allowed miners advances on the next forthcoming "half". Such advances were made in the form of scrip which was negotiable only at the company store, but allowed miners and their families to purchase food…pay the rent…and otherwise keep their heads above water until the next "half".

All advances were deducted immediately from the next paycheck, and no long term credit was allowed. This left families with little, if any, cash from one "half" to the next, resulting in continuing advances. The line, "I owe my soul to the company store!" from the song "Sixteen Tons", is a direct reference to the miners' reliance on the company store. Many miners, including Mr. Gilliam, would use any money they had remaining from their paychecks to buy moonshine whiskey and to participate in the regular Saturday night poker games.

Mr. Gilliam would play poker all night, arriving home on Sunday morning in time to bathe, shave, don his blue serge suit, grab his cap, and head out for church. He didn't miss too many church services, as he was the leader of the church choir. On one particular Sunday, Tiny's mother hid all her husband's caps before he came home from the poker game. Thus, when he was ready to leave for church, he had no cap to wear. Because Mr. Gilliam would not leave the house without a cap, Tiny's mother thought by hiding the caps, she would prevent her husband from going to church "slightly tipsy". Undaunted, Mr. Gilliam picked up his miner's helmet with the carbide lantern firmly attached. He scurried off to church. Entering the church, he saw his wife's sister, Flaura, sitting in one of the pews. He quickly deposited his helmet in her lap, saying "here, take care of this", and with equal assurance took his position in the choir.

When Tiny was 6 weeks old he contracted measles, and very rapidly developed pneumonia, which placed his life in extreme jeopardy! He was told the country doctor informed his parents that his chances for survival were very slim...but, the doctor added, there was a new drug he could try with their permission. As the story has been told, this new drug (according to the doctor) "would either cure him, or put him out of his misery." Mrs. Gilliam was reluctant, but Mr. Gilliam issued the approval. The drug was administered. Tiny never knew what drug was given to him; but suspected the drug might have been sulfa.

There is no doubt Mr. Gilliam's decision was critical to saving Tiny's life.

Due to Mr. Gilliam's penchant for drinking and gambling, several temporary splits occurred in the Gilliam marriage. Tiny vaguely remembered living a somewhat nomadic life from time to time. Mrs. Gilliam, with the three boys in tow, would visit her mother, Mam-Maw Smith in Ashland (then a town of about 20,000, nine miles west of the West Virginia state line). Mrs. Gilliam and the boys would remain in Ashland for a while. Then they'd return to Wayland for reconciliation with Mr. Gilliam. Tiny didn't know how often that scenario occurred but, when he was just past 3 years old, the split became permanent. Once more, Mrs. Gilliam and the boys headed to Ashland.

Tiny did not see much of his father after his mother moved the boys to Ashland. His father would drop by now and then, but his visits were always short, varying from 1 to 3 days, and then he would leave again. Tiny thought his father spent most of his time in southern Ohio, where he had relatives, and jobs were more plentiful. One thing Tiny remembered about his father was his burning desire for constant singing, whistling, and humming! Mr. Gilliam had a natural talent for music that never diminished. As Tiny recalled, his father once taught the subject in a rural school in Eastern Kentucky. Reportedly, Mr. Gilliam also wrote one of the hymns sung at his own funeral, "No tears in Heaven".

Another thing that mind boggled Tiny about his father was the numerous birdshot pellets visible below the skin of his arms, neck, and chest. Apparently, before Mr. Gilliam met Mrs. Gilliam, he made a trip on horseback to see a lady he had been courting. Upon arrival at her house, and before he could dismount, another suitor appeared on the front porch with a shotgun. Angered, Tiny imagined, to find his long ride had resulted in that, Mr. Gilliam drew the pistol he always carried. His horse reared just as he fired, causing him to miss his target, and his competitor "blew him out of the saddle!"

Mr. Gilliam was taken to West Liberty, Kentucky where a doctor proclaimed his wounds to be fatal, and never bothered to remove the birdshot. In time, the pellets migrated to the skin surface but since there was no pain involved, Mr. Gilliam did not consider having them removed. Tiny was fascinated being able to move those pellets around under his father's skin with his own fingers!

Tiny recalled one memorable visit he and his brothers had with their father in the early summer of 1930 (the very "pit" of the depression). Mr. Gilliam took the boys to visit their uncle, his brother Ed, who lived near West Liberty. That trip also included a very short visit with another of Mr. Gilliam's brothers, Frank, and a prolonged stay at the home of a friend in Glo. The total time the boys were with their father was almost a year. Tiny observed his 5th birthday and his father turned 50 years old during that time. Tiny remembered crying on Mr. Gilliam's birthday because he thought his father was getting so old.

During the visit with Uncle Ed, Tiny suffered a broken arm. This occurred when Tiny was carrying a child, who was a little older than him, on his back. Plaster of Paris casts for broken bones had not yet been perfected at that time. Therefore, the doctor used wooden splints to immobilize Tiny's arm. Tiny reported the procedure was very successful, as he never suffered any ill effects from the break in his later years.

Tiny did not know whether the extended trip with his father was taken with his mother's consent; but, Tiny was sure that mattered not to his father one way or the other. Neither did Tiny remember their mode of travel but, since they had no car and public transportation did not exist, he was sure they must have walked a lot. Uncle Ed had three or four boys, so Tiny and his brothers never lacked companionship during the day while the adults were hoeing corn, or clearing new ground for crops to be planted later.

One day while the adults were in the cornfield (or at least that's where Tiny and the other boys thought they were), the boys sneaked off to the watermelon patch, eagerly anticipating some very tasty...but forbidden...fruit. The boys knew the watermelon patch was "off limits" and if they were caught there, they knew they'd very likely receive a sound thrashing. That knowledge, however, did not deter the boys. They soon selected a nice ripe melon, and just as quickly, were spitting seeds. Unknown to the boys, however, the men were not in the cornfield. Instead, they were clearing higher ground and were able to see their every move.

When the hard day's work was done, the tired toilers returned to the house and washed up for supper. After everyone had gathered around the table, someone asked the boys what they had done all day. One of Tiny's cousins told the adults they had "just played games." Nothing more was said for some time. The boys thought they had pulled off stealing the watermelon. Suddenly moments later Tiny's father looked at him and said, "I bet you really did enjoy that nice watermelon, Tiny."

Caught by surprise, Tiny blurted out, "God, it sure was good."

After their visit with Uncle Ed and his family, Mr. Gilliam and the boys continued on to Glo, where they spent some time with Mr. Gilliam's friend. Tiny thought he remembered the man's name was Mister Pack, who had a son about Cliff's age. Soon after Mr. Gilliam and his sons arrived in Glo, the Gilliam boys accompanied with the Pack boy hiked into the woods in search of beech nuts (a small triangular shaped nut that is delicious and abundant in that area). Beech nuts are especially good when roasted, so the boys built a fire and proceeded to gather nuts for a feast. Needless to say, with a lot of dried leaves on the ground, the boys were really looking for a peck of trouble. Before long the fire got out of control. Knowing they could not stop the fire from spreading, the boys scurried down the hillside to safer ground. The only firefighters around were the volunteer bucket brigade. Tiny remembered the volunteer firemen were a very efficient bunch extinguishing the fire in a short time; but, not before the fire consumed a barn and fence of a local farmer. That was the only time Tiny remembered his father whipping him.

Tiny, his brothers, and their father stayed at the Pack place for some time. When the new school year started, Mr. Gilliam enrolled the boys in a one-room country school. The boys carried their lunch (called dinner in the country) in a coal miner's aluminum dinner bucket, a half round contraption, which in no way resembled the lunch pails of today. The bucket was about a foot tall with a semi-circular carrying strap riveted to each side. A very tight fitting lid covered the bucket to ensure the freshness of the contents. Tiny vividly recalled that their buckets contained buttermilk and crumbled cornbread, which was eaten with a spoon. Tiny felt there was no educational benefit to him and his brothers going to school. However, Tiny supposed his father had peace of mind knowing that as long as the boys were in school, they would not be involved in too much mischief. Since the boys did not want any part of school, especially the walking part, they skipped a lot of days.

On one occasion the boys pressed their luck a little too far, which proved to be their downfall. They had already spent the first four days of the week at their favorite spot beneath a railroad trestle. They did not complete the 5th day there, as a local townsman walking along the railroad tracks spotted them. Naturally, the townsman told Mr. Gilliam, which brought the Gilliam boys' shenanigans to a screeching halt for the remainder of the school year. The Gilliam family remained at the Pack farm until sometime in the late spring of 1931, when Mr. Gilliam got itchy feet again or, perhaps, the boys wore out their welcome. They then began the journey back to Ashland, but by a different route than what they had come.

Mr. Gilliam wanted to visit another fellow he knew on the way to Ashland. Between leaving Glo and arriving at his friend's house, they spent the night in a cornfield. The weather was very pleasant and with Tiny barefooted, somehow he stuck a piece of wire in his big toe. His father removed the wire, wiped away his tears with his bandana, and assured Tiny everything would be just fine. That calmed Tiny's fears, allowing him to fall asleep soon.

The next morning Mr. Gilliam built a fire and fixed breakfast from supplies they carried on the trip. After breakfast, Mr. Gilliam rolled each of the boys and himself a cigarette from his Prince Albert tin. Soon afterward they were on their way again.

Since planting time for some crops was still in season when the family arrived at the house of Mr. Gilliam's friend, Mr. Gilliam volunteered his and the boys' services. His friend had a peach orchard that, according to Cliff, produced great tasting peaches, which they were allowed to eat as much as they wanted; provided they planted the seed from each peach they ate. Within a few days, they were off to Ashland once more with only one more detour along the way. They stopped to see a relative living on Blaine Creek near Louisa, Kentucky in a small village about 35 miles from home. Neither Tiny nor Cliff remembered any happenings of importance at Blaine Creek. Because Tiny, his brothers, and their father were not at the relative's house very long before leaving again, Tiny believed the visit was one of those drop by and say hello kind of things. When they finally arrived in Ashland, Mr. Gilliam deposited the boys with their Mam-Maw Smith, disappearing for another 3 or 4 years.

By the time the boys arrived at their grandmother's, America was really suffering from the effects of the depression. Although Tiny was very young, he vividly recalled many of the hardships endured by his family, as well as many other families around them. Jobs were practically non-existent everywhere, especially in Ashland. Many families became totally dependent on what is known today as welfare. In those days welfare was called "relief", which was administered by the American Red Cross. No one had money. There was no money for food or rent. Evictions commonly occurred. Desperate for some way to survive, Tiny's entire family (consisting of 11 in all) joined forces and "occupied" a three-room shack bordering the city dump. There, they paid no rent. In fact, they didn't even have the owner's permission to live there. They simply assumed squatter's rights and took the place over!

Their new "home" had no running water or electricity. What were available for lighting were natural gas fixtures with mantles all over the place. They also used gas for cooking, at least for a while. Having no money with which to pay the gas bill, the company soon turned the gas off. Tiny's family turned the gas back on again. The gas company came back and removed the meter. Not to be outdone, Tiny's mother removed the plugs the company had installed and reconnected the gas using a section of tube from a bicycle tire. Eventually, the gas company got wise to what Tiny's mother was doing and turned the gas off at its source.

The Family Matriarch
Mam-Maw Smith

After the gas was permanently turned off, Mam-Maw was forced to do the cooking on the fireplace grate in the middle of the bungalow. Sometime later they managed to acquire a coal stove, allowing Mam-Maw to move her cooking skills back into the kitchen. Typically, breakfast consisted of a very high stack of "hoecakes" made from corn meal, salt, and water (in the absence of milk). The cakes were fried on top of the stove in skillets well-greased with lard. Sometimes the family was fortunate enough to have fried potatoes to supplement the tasty hoecakes, enhancing the breakfast.

After Tiny's family lost their gas "privileges", they used kerosene (called coal oil at that time) lamps for lighting. They built fires in the bedroom grates, burning wood scraps and coal stolen from the railroad, located just beyond the dump. That was the only method they had to heat the house to avoid freezing.

Tiny's family was very fortunate to have a more prosperous neighbor a few blocks away, who allowed them to fill their water buckets from his supply. All the water for cooking, drinking, bathing, and laundry had to be carried from the neighbor's place. With no bathtub, bathing was done in a metal washtub, which was also used for washing clothes. Between bodies and clothes, the tub was constantly used.

The doors and windows had no insulation. Winter winds, whistling unchallenged through the open areas, kept the family huddled around the fireplace grates a lot. At night, they stuffed gunnysacks under the doors. Broken windows were covered with cardboard. Windows not broken were never opened, since fresh air was always in plentiful supply. The roof was so full of holes they could stargaze from the comfort of their pallets and beds. When the rainy season came, all the pots, pans, the washtub, and every other container available were strategically deployed all through the house.

Fruit markets and grocery stores in those days received bananas in cone shaped crates, appropriately called banana crates. These crates were used as kitchen chairs. Bootie, somehow, became the envied owner of two banana crates. When Tiny asked him to share, Bootie flatly refused. Tiny was quick to remind Bootie that the Bible said, "If you have two coats, you should give your brother one." (Luke 3:11)

"It don't say nothin' about no banana crates," Bootie seriously replied.

So called "normal" living room furniture was not available. They had no couch, no overstuffed chair, and, of course, they had never heard of a coffee table! During daylight hours, the beds and banana crates served as chairs. The children were always reminded, "The floor is not crowded." Mam-Maw had her own personal cane bottom rocker. Heaven help anyone who got caught sitting in the rocker!

With no washer or dryer; no refrigerator; and, of course, no automobile, they had no maintenance problems. Clothes were washed on a washboard and hung outdoors to dry. Any perishables were kept in a wooden ice box, cooled by blocks of ice that cost something like a nickel for a 50-pound block. Even that posed no problem because they rarely had leftovers; thus, the iceman did not come often.

With no grass, they had no need for a lawnmower. The front yard was all dirt and cinders intermixed with weeds which were pulled when they got too high to see over. The backyard was all weeds, except for a path leading to the toilet, which was kept relatively clear by frequent trips in that direction.

The privy was located between the house and the dump. The outhouse was a "two hole" and was kept well stocked with corn cobs and Sears Roebuck catalogs. To preclude the dark and sometimes cold trips at night, chamber pots came in very handy. They called the pots "thunder mugs". Naturally, the children were given the dubious honor of emptying the pots every morning!

Sleeping quarters were two rooms off the kitchen. Due to an insufficient number of beds, pallets were placed on the floor when bed time came. Tiny, his brothers, and a cousin Jahanny (derived from James Anford) occupied one of the beds with two sleeping at the head and two at the foot. The sleeping arrangement forced all the boys to sleep facing the outside to prevent feet being in their face all night. That arrangement worked most of the time. However, an occasional "accidental" kick by a supposedly sleeping bedfellow brought out an all-out war.

As mentioned before, the house faced the city dump and nocturnal invasions by huge rats foraging for food were commonplace. The rats gained access to the house through the floor of the middle room closet. As fast as the holes were covered with a flattened tin can, the rats would gnaw another hole. Quite often the boys would awaken during the night to find a rat in or near their bed. On several occasions family members were bitten with those sleeping on the pallets most vulnerable. By the grace of God alone, no one ended up with rabies. Nor was any one seriously affected by the nocturnal visits. Most of the rats' activity was centered in the kitchen where the meager food supply was stored. Mam-Maw would enter the kitchen carrying a lighted lamp which caused the rats to scurry for their avenues of escape. Uncle Harry, armed with a rocker from an old rocking chair, would follow Mam-Maw. He clubbed as many of the rats as he could before they made their escape. Uncle Harry became very adept at swinging his rocket, often making Babe Ruth look like a rank amateur. This ritual was performed every morning before Mam-Maw mixed the ingredients for the hoecake breakfast.

The family income consisted of a $1 food voucher issued weekly by the relief program, plus $3 weekly that Tiny's mother earned as a cook at one of the local hotels. The occasional issue of commodities consisting of flour, sugar, and salt supplemented the meager income. Such was the total family resources. Meager as the provisions were, 11 people had to subsist on them. The family never ate steak. Eggs at about a penny each and milk at five cents a quart were seldom seen on the table.

Mam-Maw was never concerned about frying too many hoecakes; there was never any left. Whether she made 10 or 50, all the cakes disappeared. Unless a family person was a fast eater, that person could get left out and end up crying for more. No in-between snacks existed. Candy, soft drinks, and other goodies taken for granted today were entirely out of the question in Tiny's family.

On one occasion, Tiny was told he was crying for something to eat long before supper time. After being told by Mam-Maw she only had enough food for supper, Tiny appealed to Uncle Harry, asking him to fry him a hoecake. In an attempt to shut up Tiny, Uncle Harry said, "there's nothing in the house but some lard."

"Fry me up some of that," Tiny said. "I'm hungry!"

The boys entertained themselves. Television was then unknown and the family had no radio. The boys spent most of the daylight hours playing games…tag, marbles, Cowboys and Indians, mumble-ty-peg, and other games of the day. Organized activities were non-existent; no boys' clubs or Little League baseball. The game of marbles was probably the most popular game of the time. Both adults and children played marbles. The grown men commonly had serious competitions with the children playing marbles. Stakes ran high in some games. They always played for "keeps," meaning the winner always kept the marbles that were wagered on the game. For those who lost the marble games, the opposite was true. They "lost their marbles." Tiny remembered seeing as many as 300 or 400 marbles wagered, won or lost in a single game.

The shooting position in marbles requires both knees be firmly on the ground. Because of the wear and tear that put on clothes, Tiny's mother never approved of them playing marbles. Moreover, constant contact of the shooter's knuckles with the ground resulted in chapping and bleeding...a dead giveaway of one's participation of the game. Sympathetic to the boy's problem, Uncle Harry's wife Earl, the sister of Tiny's mother, fashioned what they called "knuxing pads" to place under the knees and knuckles.

After supper the boys played hide and seek or a game called "go-sheepie-go". Those games were subject to an early curfew. When curfew arrived, the boys were expected to be "in the house." To ensure observance of curfew, the boys were constantly reminded of the "Front Street Walker". The story, often told, about a woman who had been murdered while walking on Front Street embellished tales of her ghost returning every night sometime after dark bent on revenge for her murder. That story served to keep the children (and many adults) from sticking their heads out after 9 p.m. Keeping four rambunctious boys under control might have been more difficult without such a tale to restrain their antics. In that sense, the tale served its purpose.

During the daylight hours, Mam-Maw's favorite method of keeping tabs on the boys was to tie them to an immovable object indoors. Another one of her tactics was to make the boys wear dresses instead of the customary overalls and shirts...in the mistaken belief that embarrassment would keep the boys off the street. For the most part, this second tactic of Mam-Maw's worked. However, Jahanny was spotted more than once on the rear step of the iceman's delivery truck going down the alley with his dress flying high above his head.

The biggest problem children back then was that every adult was a disciplinarian! This was permissible and expected! Adults disciplined children when guilty of wrongdoing. Even the police officer on the beat was known to turn a mischievous lad over his knee to apply appropriate persuasion. When thrashings were called for at home, the boys were normally required to select and cut the switch with which they would be punished. Then the boys were stripped down to the bare skin. The switching lasted until blood was drawn! However, this discipline was limited to crimes of major substance. Even so, the punishment meted out in those days would be called child abuse today.

In the November, 1932 presidential election, Herbert Clark Hoover, the Republican incumbent, was soundly defeated by Franklin Delano Roosevelt, a Democrat and former Governor of New York. Roosevelt winning by such an overwhelming majority was no surprise, as the Great Depression had dramatically impacted America. Every man, woman, and child carried the mark of the depression. No one escaped the wrath of the depression. Mister Hoover bore the brunt of the blame, whether right or wrong. He was the subject of many jokes, one of which Tiny remembered very vividly:

> "Our Father who art in Heaven,
> Hoover be thy name.
> You took us off of Chesterfields,
> And put us on Golden Grain."

President Roosevelt took the oath of office in January, 1933. He immediately began introducing policies which he believed would lead the nation toward an economic recovery. One of those policies was the "New Deal", so named because when the entire banking industry collapsed (a direct result of the stock market crash October, 1929) a new deal was in order! Among other things, the New Deal created the Works Project Administration (WPA), which utilized America's men and women in a variety of jobs. Men were employed in the construction of roads, bridges, dams, schools, post offices, and other public facilities and structures. Women were employed in the manufacture of clothing for distribution to the underprivileged.

Each of Tiny's adult family members, with the exception of Mam-Maw, worked for the WPA at some time during its existence. The WPA provided a much needed shot in the arm for the economy of the nation. With the income from the resulting work people were able to buy for the first time in as much as 4 years. As this income was spent, the need for more products and services created more jobs. This put more money into circulation, allowing the private business sector to make a much needed recovery. With jobs more plentiful, the WPA workers were able to lay down their picks and shovels, or their needles and thread, to get better paying jobs keeping more within their abilities and desires.

The improved economy allowed "blended" families such as Tiny's to abandon the communal living style they had adopted out of dire necessity. Uncle Harry was hired by a local scrap metal processing company, a forerunner of the modern recycling station. That allowed him and Aunt Earl to leave the nest. Both Aunt Phoebe and Aunt Flaura both remarried. Along with their new husbands, and children, Betty Jean and Jahanny, respectively, they were able to set up separate housekeeping. Mam-Maw moved in with Phoebe and her family. Then Tiny, his brothers, and their mother moved from their one time rat infested "haven". By 1934 the rats had the place all to themselves. During the next few years Tiny and his family lived several places, including in Ashland; in Catlettsburg, Kentucky; and, in Huntington, West Virginia. Their frequent moves were primarily prompted by Tiny's mother changing jobs. She always tried to upgrade the family's standard of living.

The depression years, Tiny believed, were a definite blot on America's history. He often said that if times like those should occur again in his lifetime, his family would not go hungry like his family in his childhood often did. Tiny said he would first make every effort to work to support his family. If unable to work for any reason, he would resort to other measures—begging, borrowing, or stealing! No doubt Tiny would have done anything and everything necessary to assure the survival of his family.

***

CHAPTER 2

The School Years

At the beginning of the 1932 school year Tiny and his cousin Jahanny (9 days Tiny's junior) were enrolled in grade 1-B at Wylie Elementary School. Wylie school occupied one square block, bounded by Winchester Avenue on the south, Greenup Avenue on the north, and 31st and 32nd streets to the east and west. The school was merely a stone's throw away from the boys' house by the dump. Thus, the boys could walk to school. The school had no kindergarten or other preschool activity. Other than Tiny's short school attendance in Glo, this was a brand new ball game for the two wide-eyed 7-year-old boys.

The only previous exposure to the outside world for Tiny and Jahanny was an occasional trip downtown with an adult family member. They soon discovered that children from the more affluent parts of town had a somewhat different standard of living than what they had ever experienced. The more fortunate school children did not wear patched overalls, shoes with holes and cardboard insoles, and sockless feet like Tiny, his cousin, and their friends in the immediate neighborhood of the dump.

When lunch time came, the children living in the neighborhood of the dump were the only ones to remove cold corn bread from paper lunch sacks. With

The School Years

skim milk provided by the relief organization they washed down the corn bread. Having the skim milk to drink was a treat to the less fortunate children since they rarely received such a luxury.

Cliff and Bootie were already in attendance at Wylie. Compared to Tiny and Jahanny, they were old pros at the new game the younger boys were learning. The older boys had accustomed themselves to the routine of having to ask permission to go to the inside toilet at school and of not being able to go outside to play, except at recess. Always adding "Mam" to every "yes" and "no" had become the standard for the older boys. The younger boys were about to learn!

What Tiny liked most about his new adventure was the kindness shown by Mrs. Hill, the school principal. His 1st grade teacher, Mrs. James, also was nice but Mrs. Hill was a "very special lady" throughout Tiny's days in Ashland. Her husband was a river boat captain on the Ohio River. After Tiny returned from the Navy years later, Mr. Hill offered to train Tiny to take over when he retired.

The first 4 years of school for Tiny were routine, everyday occurrences that all children go through at that age, with one exception. When Tiny was in the 3rd or 4th grade, a girl, who had a brother a year or two older than Tiny, began bringing clothing to school to give Tiny. She brought pants, shirts, jackets, sweaters, and more. Tiny soon became the best dressed child in his neighborhood. He remembered a tweed suit with "knickers". Tiny thought he was hot stuff when he wore the suit. He was really proud when he attended the church revival meetings on the Wylie school grounds all decked out in those knickers.

Ashland is located in what is known as the Ohio River Valley. At that time an airport sat north of Ashland. Beyond the airport flowed the river. Wooded hills bordered the south side of Ashland back then. Though forbidden to do so, as Tiny and his playmates grew older (and bolder), they began to frequent the river for fishing, swimming and sunning. Because the hills were not off limits, they spent many hours there in the summer gathering blackberries, walnuts, and papaws. In winter the snow surfaces of the roads and embankments were ideal for sledding. Although the boys had no sleds, cardboard boxes made good substitutes.

Another popular place among the hills was what the boys called "Cliffside Caves", a favorite spot for children to play. Once when Tiny was in the 5th grade, he went with a friend and the friend's older brother to the caves. For some reason known only to the older boy, he decided to dislodge a large boulder that rolled down the hill towards Winchester Avenue. The boulder crashed into one of the homes located at the foot of the hill, doing considerable damage, including the destruction of a refrigerator. No one was home at the time so no personal injuries occurred.

Fleeing the area, the boys were spotted by someone who recognized them and called the police. The following Monday from his classroom, Tiny saw a police car pull up. He wondered *why*. His answer was not long in coming. Soon the three boys were summoned to the principal's office to be confronted with their deed. They were not taken into custody, but were ordered to appear at the county court house in Catlettsburg to be confronted by a black robed judge. To say Tiny was scared stiff to be standing before that judge would be a gross understatement! Because of their age, Tiny and his friend were let off with a stern warning. The older boy was sentenced and served a week in the county jail.

The Gillum boys' favorite river spot was a secluded area they called 29th Street beach. The immediate approach was surrounded by trees, which provided an "early warning system". On a rotation basis, one boy was always stationed in the tallest tree, which provided an excellent view of the area. When unwelcomed visitors approached, the boy standing guard would sound a warning, and the rest of the boys scurried for cover until the one on watch sounded the "all clear" signal.

The river in that area had a sandy bottom. For about 50 yards out, the water was only 3 to 4 feet deep—ideal conditions for swimming. Once a boy who could not swim too well ventured out to where the water was over his head. Fortunately nearby, Tiny towed the boy to safety. The boy committed the unpardonable sin by telling his mother Tiny had saved his life. His mother was so grateful that she came over to Tiny's house to tell his mother how proud she should be of Tiny. Tiny's mother expressed her pleasure by giving her son a very hard switching (for being at the river). Needless to say, the Gillum boys' swimming trips were put on hold for a while.

Periodically, the Ashland City Health Department promoted various health programs. Medical personnel would visit the various schools to provide physical examinations, including chest x-rays, at no cost. Abnormalities, if any, also were treated free of charge. One of the health issues the medical personnel promoted was dental hygiene. On one occasion, each student was given a toothbrush, a tube of toothpaste, and a chart on which brushings were to be recorded. Being the nearest thing to candy the Gillum boys had seen in a long while, they ate the toothpaste and threw away the toothbrush and chart. An award was given to those students who completed the project. Obviously, the Gillum boys were not part of the awards ceremony. Neither were they invited to participate in any future similar projects. Examinations by qualified medical personnel were an entirely new experience for the Gillum brothers. Tiny remembered only rarely being treated by a doctor in his early life.

Mam-Maw had her own remedies—castor oil, Epsom salts, sassafras tea, and asafetida, to name a few. Castor oil and Epsom salts were given on a regular basis as laxatives, whether needed or not. These home remedies made very effective substitute laxatives. Sassafras tea, brewed from bark peeled from sassafras bushes, was a cure-all tonic and administered quite frequently. Sassafras yields a substance called saffrole, which has been identified as a carcinogen and banned for use in foods and beverages in the United States. Tiny felt lucky that none of the family suffered any ill effects from the home remedies that Mam-Maw used.

Asafetida (we called it "fetida") is a foul smelling gum obtained from various plants of the parsley family. Mam-Maw put the gum in a small bag, such as Bull Durham tobacco sacks, which were abundant in those days. Then she put the bag on a string for the boys to wear around their neck to repel all kinds of disease. Tiny wasn't sure how well the gum repelled disease, but the foul smell sure repelled friends and neighbors!

Most of Mam-Maw's remedies were effective. For example, Tiny was subject to frequent nosebleeds. For no apparent reason, the blood would flow. Sometimes strong measures were required to stem the flow of blood. Once while in school, Tiny's nose began bleeding profusely. At school they packed his nose with cotton. Tiny swore they stuffed a small bale up his nostrils. At home Mam-Maw proclaimed that she would "cure" Tiny of his nosebleeds.

First, Mam-Maw hammered a small piece of lead into a flat "coin" about one half inch in diameter and a sixteenth of an inch in thickness. She then pierced the lead coin, laced a string through the coin, and ordered Tiny to wear the coin around his neck 24 hours a day, 7 days a week. Tiny didn't remember how long he wore that amulet; but, his nosebleeds stopped!

Since Tiny's family moved on a regular basis, all of Tiny's grade school days were not spent at Wylie. He believed he attended a total of six schools in Ashland. He remembered attending at least three of these schools on various occasions.

While attending Bayless School at the west end of town, Tiny was given his first assignment of responsibility beyond normal homework assignments. Boys served as crossing guards in a group called "patrol boys", headed by a captain, with a lieutenant as second in command. Being named to the patrol boys was an honor. When Tiny's badge proclaimed him to be a lieutenant, he considered this a singular token of honor.

In addition to acting as crossing guards, the patrol boys were charged with patrolling the school grounds and areas nearby. They were charged with reporting misconduct such as fighting, swearing, and smoking. Being an "enforcer", Tiny thought the rules did not apply to him. Thus, when invited into the alley to smoke a cigarette with a friend, Tiny accepted the invitation. After all, Tiny had been smoking since he was 9 years old! As everyone knows, what goes around comes around, and in doing so Tiny had his first lesson in psychological strategy. When someone reported Tiny's infraction to the principal, being a very wise (and kind) lady, she called the patrol boys to her office as a group. She announced, "It has been brought to my attention that one of you boys has been smoking in the alley....."

With the principal's announcement Tiny's heart did several flip-flops, probably skipping a beat or two while he agonized over the fate about to befall him. After a brief pause (that seemed forever to Tiny), she continued by saying "...but, I have dismissed this report, as I am sure NONE of you boys would do such a thing. Now, go on back to your classes, and keep up the good work."

Tiny had no doubt that the principal knew he was the guilty party. Her choice of psychology over disciplinary action did Tiny a world of good. Thereafter, Tiny broke no more rules, becoming a dedicated patrol boy. Unfortunately, Tiny was unable to complete the term at Bayless because his family moved back to the east end of Ashland,

Back at Wylie in grade 5-A, Tiny became interested in baseball. Back then schools had no sports programs like those available today. Boys who played relied on the YMCA for league formation, schedules, and umpires. Leagues, as such, were divided by age. Tiny joined a group of 12 and 13-year-old boys. Their team, the Wildcats, was entered in the Midget League. At that time parents were not involved, which Tiny thought should probably be the case today. The ball players then had no adult coaches with little supervision.

Whether due to majority vote or lack of interest from other team members, Tiny became the Wildcats' manager. As if being saddled with a child as manager was not bad enough, the Wildcats operated with an additional handicap, which other teams in their league did not have to contend with. The Wildcats had no equipment or money to purchase equipment. Among the 10 or 12 children on the roster, only one (the 1st baseman) owned a glove.

A local semi-pro team gave the Wildcats their broken bats, which were repaired with nails and tape. The catcher for the Wildcats wore no protective equipment. Unless opponent teams loaned the Wildcats their gloves, the team members played barehanded!

Four teams comprised the Midget League. In addition to the Wildcats, Ashland had one other entry, a team sponsored by a local grocer. The remaining two teams were from Westwood and Flatwoods, both small towns outside of Ashland. Games were played on the only diamond in Central Park, which served the needs of everyone...children and adults!

In addition to managing the Wildcats, Tiny also served as the team's pitcher because no one else on the team showed any interest in pitching. As they say, "It's a tough job, but somebody has to do it."

One other team player sometimes relieved Tiny as a pitcher when he was getting pounded too much. Although not having adults involved had advantages, disadvantages also existed, which proved hazardous in some ways. No records were kept of innings pitched, number of pitches in a game, or rest between starts. In those areas, the players certainly could have used adult supervision.

Tiny was uncertain as to where he learned his little pitching knowledge; but, he developed a "drop" (now called a sinker) and two curve balls, overhand and sidearm. The sidearm curve ball proved to be Tiny's downfall. The unnatural elbow movement required by a sidearm curve caused bone chips that restricted the use of his elbow the rest of his life.

Although the Wildcats were not properly coached, supervised, nor managed, they did win the league championship every year they played in the Midget League, and later, in the older Junior League. Two of the Wildcats' players later signed contracts with Major League farm teams.

One of Tiny's most vivid recollections occurred two winters before his great love affair with baseball began. Due to heavy rains in the fall of 1936, the Ohio River overflowed January, 1937, creating one of the nation's most disastrous floods. Tiny's family lived in an apartment above a grocery store then. Before the river crested, water rose more than halfway up the outside stairs leading to their apartment.

The 1937 Flood in Ashland, KY
Photo Retrieved from
http://kykinfolk.org/kyboyd/Photographs/Flood/1937/flood1937.htm

The School Years

Tiny's family was spared damage, but was forced to evacuate, and wait for the waters to recede. Riding a rowboat to higher ground was an experience Tiny never forgot. His family, like many others from flooded areas, had no place to go. Churches in Ashland opened their doors to the displaced families, rich or poor, and provided them with food and shelter. Tiny and his family were fed and housed at the Church of God.

Photo Retrieved From
http://kykinfolk.org/kyboyd/Photographs/Flood/1937/flood1937.htm

Meals were brought in to the churches and served military style using trays. Tiny thought he remembered his brother Bootie discovering that the food being served at the First Christian Church (about 2 blocks away) was "tastier and more plentiful". Therefore, the Gillum boys scurried over there at mealtimes.

The family returned to their place of residence only after the flood waters receded and cleanup began. Tons of mud and debris had to be removed

Photo Retrieved From
http://kykinfolk.org/kyboyd/Photographs/Flood/1937/flood1937.htm

from the ground floor residences before damages could be repaired. Most furniture and appliances were beyond repair and had to be discarded. A federally funded assistance program was established to help those in need. Since Tiny, his brothers, and their mother lived on the second floor, they were spared damage to any personal belongings. However, other members of their clan and many of their friends lost everything. The government program helped those families to start over. Soon afterward several giant flood walls were constructed. These walls have been a major factor in controlling the mighty Ohio River.

After the flood the family moved to a location on Front Street between 29th and 30th Streets. The porch was only about 40 feet from the railroad tracks. At Christmas time, the engineers, firemen, and other crew members would throw sacks of candy on or near the porch. The Gillum boys were like a bunch of vultures each time a train passed!

Once a shirttail relative came by to visit and gave each of the boys a penny. Tiny could hardly wait for the store to open next morning so he could buy candy. A penny back then was equivalent to a $1 in today's world because seeing that much money was rare for the boys. The only time they had anything more than their sometimes daily bread was when they stole. The Gillum boys stole fruit from the open air markets, apples and cherries from the fruit trees of local citizens, and cinnamon rolls from the local bakery.

The bakers deposited their baked goods on open racks in a loading area at the back of the bakery. Although enclosed, the overhead doors stood open so trucks could back in for loading. The boys learned how to sneak in and fill their pockets (and mouths). However, one evening the boys must have been expected. Just as they were helping themselves to their cinnamon rolls…which, by the way, were very large and covered with lots of icing…they heard a noise. Someone was closing the overhead door to trap them inside. Fortunately for the boys, the door was operated by hand. Before the man could close the door entirely, the boys were gone! Tiny was the last one to get out, having to make a dive under the door, which, by then, could not have been no more than 1 or 2 feet from the floor. Pete Rose would have been proud of Tiny for that headfirst slide! That, of course, was the Gillum boys' last visit to the bakery!

Tiny and one of his friends had a close call once. They decided to climb a cherry tree and feast on the ripened fruit in a citizen's backyard. Thinking the owner was not at home, they were positioned in the tree eating the delicious cherries when a man came out the door to retrieve some clothes left on the line to dry. The two boys held their breath, hoping to not get caught, while the man gathered his clothes and went back indoors. Fate had other plans! Just as the man neared his door, the tree branch on which Tiny was sitting gave way causing him to tumble to the ground. As Tiny scrambled to his feet, his friend dropped down, and the two were off and running. The man was so surprised that he made no attempt to chase the boys. Of course, at the moment, the boys were not looking back!

After graduating from the 6th grade, Tiny enrolled in Coles Junior High School a major milestone for him. At Coles, Tiny learned mathematics instead of arithmetic, and literature instead of reading. Several manual training classes (precursor to vocational training) also were offered at the junior high level, along with social and general sciences. For a 13-year-old somewhat introverted lad, the change proved to be quite a culture shock. By then, Cliff and Bootie had quit school. They were working at a local café to help support the family. That gave Tiny incentive to continue his education with hopes of getting a better job when his school days were over.

One elective Tiny took was a shop class. The teacher was coach of the "B" football team (comparable to the junior varsity today). He was a tough talking, tough acting, overbearing individual who left no doubt as to "who" was going to be the "boss". To get the students' attention, he used a wooden pointer (which was always in his hand)—not for pointing, but as a weapon! He frequently rapped inattentive students on the side of the head with that pointer. One day Tiny and another boy were enjoying some good natured horseplay while the teacher's back was turned. He saw nothing; only heard the boys. He turned and strode directly toward Tiny, delivering a resounding blow to the side of Tiny's head.

Unaffected by the fact that he was guilty, Tiny thought the teacher acted improperly by singling him out and punishing him without so much as a question. As a response, as soon as Tiny started back toward the front of the class, he picked up another one of the teacher's pointers from a nearby chalk tray and returned the blow. Tiny hit the teacher hard enough to cause the pointer to shatter into what seemed to be a million pieces. Tiny ran to escape the teacher's wrath. However, the principal called Tiny to his office later, which resulted in Tiny's being permanently ejected from any of the teacher's classes. To substitute for the class, Tiny was placed in study hall, which worked to his advantage because he could usually complete all his homework during school hours, leaving after school for baseball.

After school one would find Tiny playing baseball, reading about the game, or listening to the games on the radio. For no other reason that Tiny could think of other than living about 150 miles from Cincinnati, Ohio, he adopted the Cincinnati baseball as his National League team. At that time, Tiny began rooting for "the Reds" and never stopped for the rest of his life. When later, the New York Yankees played an exhibition game in Ashland; Tiny chose that team as his American League team.

The Reds' home games were broadcast live, while their games played out of town were recreated. An announcer in the Cincinnati studio received play by play descriptions via telegraph (called ticker tape). From these accounts, the announcer recreated the game, adding sound effects, including fan noise. This was updated at the end of each half inning. Tiny wasn't bothered by the fact that the details were delayed. He had no other way to get the games, especially any time sooner.

Pool halls also had ticker tapes and posted inning by inning scores for all Major League games on huge blackboards. Though illegal, bets were placed at the pool halls. If anyone wanted "action", the pool halls were the place to go.

The Reds, like most of the baseball teams of the day, had lots of talent. This was long before anyone thought of expansion. Only eight teams existed in each league at that time. The playoff format of today had not been developed. The winners in each league met in the World Series. The winner there was crowned "champions". Some Reds pitching names of the time were Bucky Walters, Paul Derringer, and Johnny Vandermeer (a hard throwing lefthander). Ernie Lombardi was the catcher, Frank McCormick played 1st base, and a pretty fair outfielder name Wally Post patrolled left field.

Back then, pitchers threw every 3rd day. However, relief pitching, though available, was not as specialized as today. The Reds did have a couple of good pitchers in Gene Thompson and "fireman" Joe Beggs. In 1939 the Reds won the National League pennant; but were swept in four games by the Yankees in the World Series. Prophetically, the Reds said, "Wait until next year." In 1940 the Reds captured the pennant and went on to sweep the Detroit Tigers in four games.

Movies were another favorite pastime for Tiny. Ashland had four theatres; but only two of them were remotely in his price range. The Lyric and The Grand charged a dime, while the price of admission at The Capitol and The Paramount was a quarter. Anytime the Gilliam brothers could scrape up a dime, they arrived at one of the theaters by 9 AM when the doors opened. Usually there was a double feature western, a serial, comedy, and a cartoon. They often stayed to see the entire bill two or more times. For lunch they carried a bologna sandwich to tide them over until supper. Sometimes when the boys didn't have a dime, they would sneak into the theater. On such occasions the boys waited for the ending of the first presentation, mingling with the exiting crowd, slowly working their way through the exit doors. Surprisingly enough, the boys were often successful.

Soon Tiny received the opportunity to get his first job. With Ashland having no school bus service, Tiny walked to school. The route he traveled took Tiny by a Mom and Pop grocery store. One morning the owner offered Tiny a job sweeping the store and the sidewalk in front of the store. He was required to perform his duties twice a day, going to and from school. Paying $1 a week, the job made Tiny feel as if he had conquered the world. Later the owner expanded Tiny's duties, allowing him to serve kids at the candy counter when he was busy with adult customers. Although Tiny was spending more time on the job, he received no pay increase, which mattered not to Tiny. The only reward Tiny needed was seeing his friends "green with envy"! On occasion the store owner generously gave Tiny a piece of candy. This too pleased Tiny! He worked for the grocer until he graduated from Coles.

In 1939, with war in Europe, all signs led to America's eventual involvement. By this time, the nation's economy was much improved in large part due to programs implemented by Roosevelt's administration's New Deal. One program that developed out of the New Deal was the Civilian Conservation Corps (CCC). A military type organization, the CCC put thousands of young men aged 17 through 20 to work in forestry and other public works projects.

Members of the CCC lived in army style barracks, wore uniforms, and were governed by military like regulations. Enlistments were for periods of 6 months; although, resignations were allowed for family hardships and other valid reasons. Pay was $13 a month for a first enlistment. Thereafter, pay increased to $16. Like the military, clothing, food, shelter, and medical services were included.

Both Bootie and Cliff enlisted in the CCC. They were told they could select the geographical area in which they would serve. Thinking they might escape the harsh Kentucky winters and wanting to see new lands, they asked for the Western United States. Therein they found another similarity to military service. They were sent west alright—about 60 miles to Morehead, Kentucky! Bootie stuck out the CCC for one enlistment. However, Cliff, concluding the CCC was not his "cup of tea", resigned to come home to Ashland before his enlistment ended.

Though Ashland was not typical of the larger cities, the town had its traditions. One such tradition was the celebration of Halloween. Festivities began at dusk and continued to midnight or later. Every year people came from all parts of town and elsewhere to watch and/or participate in the "Halloween walk". Men, women, boys, and girls of all ages and sizes forsook other activities to join this annual event. The walk began at the corner of 16th Street and Winchester Avenue, paraded around a 4 square block area, and featured costumes of all kinds, mostly homemade. Marchers were four abreast and "bumper to bumper", so to speak, like modern day freeways. Although there were no dignitaries on hand with canned speeches, everyone had lots of fun.

The School Years

On Halloween evening there were other traditional happenings. Porch swings found their way to the top of telephone poles, outhouses somehow got flipped over, soaped windows, and raw corn mysteriously appeared on people's porches—these were the "trick" part of Ashland's Halloween celebration then. The "walk" was the treat. By comparison to "trick or treat" activities today with children exposed to many hazards, children of that era were certainly in a more secure and happier place and time.

May 21, 1941 Tiny graduated from Coles Junior High. The first of Tiny's family to ever graduate from anything, this was quite an achievement. Tiny felt proud and looked forward to high school. However, he did not know then that "the best laid plans of mice and men" often go awry, which he would soon learn.

As always, the summer after his junior high graduation, Tiny spent the summer months playing baseball, sneaking off to the river and, otherwise, just goofing off. In September Tiny joined other eager and not so eager students choosing classes for the fall term. With few electives, most classes were mandatory, including biology. When Tiny was told he would have to enroll in biology, the desire for higher education suddenly abandoned him. He had no desire to dissect bugs, or do other things he thought to be disgusting. Tiny wasn't sure whether his intense dislike of biology, the new surroundings, or the new routines led to his dropping out of school. Whatever the cause, at the end of 1 week as a sophomore, Tiny's school days ended.

***

CHAPTER 3

World War II...Stateside

"A DATE THAT WILL LIVE IN INFAMY," President Roosevelt said, characterizing December 7, 1941. On that fateful Sunday morning Japan, without warning, bombed the United States Naval Base at Pearl Harbor on the coast of Oahu, Hawaii. Japan's actions plunged America headlong into World War II.

At the time America entered WWII one of Tiny's friends owned a bob-tailed terrier that would rather kill rats than eat the most sumptuous dog food. The teenager boys only had to say, "Let's go get a rat, Bob", and the dog was ready and willing. On that particular morning that Pearl Harbor was bombed the boys were rat hunting by the Ohio River, where larger rats could be found. Bob killed 16 rats that day. Later Tiny thought many times how appropriate for them to be killing rats at home while "rats" were bombing Pearl Harbor.

The sneak attack on Pearl Harbor was very costly to the United States in terms of personnel, in addition to aircraft and naval vessels. Although reeling from these losses, the entire country rallied behind Roosevelt, accepting the many sacrifices necessary to mount an all-out offensive. Everyone knew this would lead to the beginning of the end for Japanese Emperor Hirohito and his military forces.

Due to the prudent forethought of President Roosevelt, America made giant strides in the buildup of its armed forces. The Selective Service Act, introduced and passed by Congress in 1940, required all men in the 20 to 40 age group to immediately register for the military draft. Requirements were later changed to make registering for the draft for males mandatory upon reaching his 18th birthday. By December 1941 America's previously all volunteer (1939) military force of 200,000 men had increased to

1,640,000, giving the United States a formidable military force for that era.

Barely 4 months past his 16th birthday, Tiny was caught between a rock and a hard spot. He was not only too young for military service; he was too young to work for the defense plants that began gearing up for the war effort. About that time another New Deal spinoff, the National Youth Administration (NYA), began accepting 17 year olds in various training programs. The NYA conducted classes in welding, machine shop, sheet metal, and electrical trades. Follow-up to the NYA training courses was job placement in places such as Baltimore, Maryland; Detroit, Michigan; and Dayton, Ohio, to name a few.

Not yet 17 years old, Tiny lied about his age and was accepted into one of the NYA programs. With most trainees a school dropout, the NYA established a regular school curriculum. Regulations mandated each participant to work 4 hours in the shops and to attend school 4 hours per day Monday through Friday of each week. A normal course lasted 16 weeks. When Tiny completed his course, he still was not old enough for job placement. However, due to a very understanding instructor who taught his class, Tiny was allowed to repeat the course.

By the time his 2nd session was completed, Tiny was old enough to qualify for job placement. The Glenn L. Martin Aircraft Company of Baltimore contacted Tiny for a job interview. Tiny considered this an ideal situation as both Bootie and Cliff had already been processed through the NYA program and were working for the Martin Company.

The State of Maryland at that time required anyone who wanted to accept employment in that state to have been a resident of the state for a minimum of 30 days. A "resident camp" had been established in Beltsville (a suburb of Baltimore) where NYA graduates were required to live while completing their residence requirements. Tiny and others who stayed at the camp lived in barracks, ate in chow halls, and continued training for their chosen occupations. During the 30 days Tiny spent in Beltsville he gained valuable experience that would pay off in the days to come.

The morning Tiny boarded the bus for Baltimore was a memorable event. Tiny was in disbelief that a small town boy like him was on his way to the big city and beginning a career in the fabulous aircraft industry. That was the 1st time he had been in a town larger than Huntington, West Virginia (a larger town near Ashland, but certainly no metropolis). So excited taking in the sights, Tiny completely forgot to notify his brothers of his arrival!

The Glenn L. Martin Company was located just outside Baltimore in Dundalk close to the main streetcar line. Though an old country boy, Tiny had no problem boarding the streetcar, dropping in a dime, and being on the way to the interview he had looked forward to for such a long time. At the personnel office Tiny completed the necessary forms and then joined a long line of others waiting their turn for interviews. With the lines moving quickly, Tiny soon found himself answering questions about personal history and past experience. He was absolutely certain that his "vast" sheet metal experience would land him a job in the sheet metal department. Wrong!

Company representatives offered Tiny a job as an apprentice tube bender on the 2nd shift at 60 cents an hour. Tiny was very surprised that his employers did not see him fit to use in the skills for which he had been trained. However, back then $24 pay for 40 hours work was not too shabby. They paid time and a half for all hours worked on Saturday (which turned out to be every Saturday).

Tiny could not believe he would be earning 60 cents an hour, much less the 90 cents an hour for overtime. He was elated when he rushed to a telephone and told the operator to give him Boulevard 142, the telephone number of the residence where his brother Cliff rented a sleeping room. The landlord answered the phone to inform Tiny his brother had already left for work, as he too was working the 2nd shift. Fortunately, the landlord had been told Tiny was coming and was kind enough to go to the Martin Company to give him a ride to the rooming house.

Prior to Tiny's arrival in Baltimore, Bootie was married and had already moved from the rooming house. Tiny conveniently took over his bed and began paying the $3 per week for rent. For another $7, Tiny was served three meals a day at a boarding house a short distance from his sleeping quarters. With no income taxes deducted and very low Social Security contributions, most of Tiny's $31.20 was take home pay. After paying the $10 for room and board and sending his mother $10, Tiny still had over $10 for transportation and other necessities, which was more than sufficient.

The tubing department employed about 60 people, plus the supervisory staff. Of this total, most employees were female. By then the draft had taken a toll on the male employees, leaving the manufacturing of aircraft to "Rosie the riveter", and her cohorts. In addition to Tiny, then 17 years old, and the supervisors, only two other males worked in the tubing department. One of those males was a young man in his 20's waiting for Uncle Sam's call. The other male was a 42-year-old gentleman who, of course, was too old for the draft.

World War II...Stateside

The Martin Company was a sprawling complex, occupying many acres of land. The one thing Tiny remembered most about the place was the manner in which the entire facility was camouflaged. The huge parking lots were covered with special netting. All the buildings were painted colors that blended in with the surrounding area, making the view from the air very deceiving.

At that time, Martin produced three types of aircraft: the PBM Mariner, a seaplane for the Navy; the B-26, an Air Force bomber; and, a fighter/bomber simply designated the 187, which was funded by the British and dubbed "the flying whore". Although the surroundings in the tubing department were quite different than those he had worked in sheet metal shops previously, Tiny adapted rapidly. He soon learned to operate the various machines used in bending, beading, and flaring tubes of all sizes that were manufactured for installation in the aircraft. After a short time, Tiny's assignment became mock-up operations, which required the hand forming of tubing small enough in diameter to be used as a pattern in the development of the "real thing" that was contractually required to be installed on the aircraft. Once this "pattern" had been Company Engineer and Customer Approved, mass production of the "real thing" could then be accomplished. This was a welcomed departure from the monotonous hours on the bending machines.

In September, 1942, hardly a month into Tiny's new job, he and his brothers received word that their father had been hit by a car and killed while walking along one of the state highways outside Franklin, Ohio. The three brothers took a leave of absence from the Martin Company to attend their father's funeral in New Boston, Ohio. Even though the brothers had not seen their father very often as a child and had not seen him in many months prior to his death, Tiny found the funeral and subsequent burial rites very sad. Later Tiny often wondered how his life might have been different to have grown up with a full-time father. Clearly, the depression years might not have been significantly different financially, but the emotional impact of the depression might have proved less traumatic by his father's presence.

After their father's funeral, Cliff, Bootie, and Tiny spent a couple days with their mother before returning to Baltimore for their jobs. Soon afterward, Cliff's draft notice arrived. In November 1942 Cliff headed to basic training with the Army Corps of Engineers. Although registered for the draft, Bootie's being married and a father delayed the receipt of his "Greetings" from "Uncle Sam" for some time. However, he was eventually called to become a sailor. As for Tiny, he would have joined the Navy at age 17 had he been old enough. At 17 years old, he needed his mother's permission. Like most mothers, her response to Tiny's request was "when hell freezes over."

After Cliff departed for the Army, Tiny moved in with Bootie and his wife, Dorothy. They only lived a few blocks from the rooming house.

The draft rapidly depleted the nation's male population and drained industry of its skilled workers. The Selective Service System was then altered to allow deferment of some married men, in particular fathers, from the system. Certain other skilled workers also were eligible for deferment if their employer could show that difficulty in replacing them would adversely affect the production of war materials.

The Martin Company immediately began processing deferment requests, including Tiny's. That did not fit Tiny's plans! Unable to gain parental consent to join the Navy, he was only waiting to be drafted. If Tiny quit his job he risked not being eligible for hiring by another company because the defense industry would not hire a person without a "release" from any former employer. Furthermore, if Tiny quit his job, he still wasn't old enough to enlist in the Navy without his mother's consent. He had no choice but to work until drafted.

By mid-1943, Tiny was concerned about how to get into the Navy to perform what he believed was his "patriotic duty". To request a "release", Tiny went to his foreman with a concocted story about his mother being sick and with Cliff being in the service, there was no one else to care for her. At the termination interview, Tiny related how he would like to seek work closer to home to care for his mother. The combination of Tiny's sad story and an understanding boss did the trick. Tiny's release was granted!

Ashland had no job opportunities. That was okay with Tiny, as Baltimore had more appeal to him for many reasons, including the company of a girl he had been dating. Thus, his job search was confined to Baltimore. Tiny needed to find a temporary job to subsist while waiting for his induction notice. With only 3 months to wait for draft registration, any job accepted at that point would not qualify Tiny for deferment. Applying at the Maryland Drydock Company, a shipbuilding and repair facility revealed that 18 was their minimum hiring age. Employers there said they would keep Tiny's application for hiring after July 28. That was Tiny's first encounter with "don't call us, we'll call you."

With Tiny restricted to public transportation having to walk about a mile to the nearest street car terminal, locating temporary employment proved to be quite frustrating for him. Limited to classified ads in the Baltimore Sun, many attempts were fruitless for Tiny. Finally, the Pennsylvania Railroad advertised a job opening on the 2nd shift with no experience required and a minimum age of 17. The pay would be no more than what Tiny had received at the Martin Company. However, the position was exactly what Tiny needed.

Railroad cars were equipped with waste boxes containing yarn like material soaked in oil. Friction from braking generates heat. Thus, the yarn like material had to be changed frequently to minimize fire hazards. However, frequent fires still occurred. Tiny's job was to replace the material in the "hot boxes", after first extinguishing the flame. Tiny and his co-workers had no fire extinguishers then. They had to extinguish fires by using heavy gloves to literally smother the flames, remove the old material, install new material, and then move on to the next hot box.

Finally, Tiny's 18th birthday, July 28, a Wednesday, arrived. One excited young fellow, Tiny, who had counted the days for almost 2 years anticipating this event, walked in to register for the draft at Towson, Maryland. Tiny's permanent place of residence was still listed in Ashland at that time. Thus, Tiny became a part of Kentucky's draft quota. Because of the population difference and the lack of critical industries in Ashland, Tiny's induction was no doubt accelerated.

The National Selective Service headquarters defined and uniformly applied the selection process for the draft. Local draft boards established and supervised implementation of quotas. The process was divided into 5 stages:

1. Occupational Questionnaire

World War II...Stateside

2. Selective Service Questionnaire
3. Notification of Draft Classification
4. Requirement to Report for Blood Testing
5. Notice to Report for Induction (also known as GREETINGS! because the salutation in the notice began with "Greetings, you have been chosen by your friends and neighbors...")

Surprisingly, a few days after Tiny registered for the draft, the Maryland Drydock Company called him to work. Termination of Tiny's railroad employment and accepting the new position resulted in a slight increase in pay. His job was to make repairs to Liberty ships returning from the war zones. This entailed repairing or replacing bulkheads, ventilation ducts, and other structural components damaged in battle. During this time Tiny's desire to be a sheet metal worker came to pass. Because of the various types of damage, the work was never boring.

Regarding the draft selection process, deadlines for completion of the selective service and occupational questionnaires existed. Although ample time was provided, Tiny completed and returned his forms no later than the day he received them. This may not have been a record; but, no doubt, Tiny's promptness accelerated his induction. One month from the day Tiny registered, August 28, his "greetings" arrived!

Tiny was ordered to report to Huntington, West Virginia (the induction site for Ashland and vicinity) September 7, 1943. He then terminated his employment, said goodbye to his Baltimore friends, made a last quick visit home, and then went to war! Tiny was truly excited!

While in Ashland, Tiny met the high school baseball coach on the street. Although Tiny was never a member of his team, the coach had befriended him, and gave him some much appreciated advice. After the exchange of pleasantries, Tiny told the coach he was reporting for induction in a few days. Revealing what a small world Tiny lived in, he learned the coach was a member of the local draft board, one of the "friends and neighbors" who had selected him.

When the coach asked Tiny his preference, he told him the Navy. Then, without any hesitation, the coach said, "Then you had better tell them you want the Army!" Tiny then questioned the coach's wise advice. The coach reassured Tiny, saying "Believe me, if you want the Navy, you had better not tell them so, because you will not like their response!"

Induction Tuesday arrived. Tiny along with dozens of other would be heroes departed the local American Legion hall on a bus. They were dropped at the Huntington Armory. The inductees stood in line to answer a barrage of questions about work experience, education, and other matters. Tiny didn't get past the preliminary information desk! Somehow, stage 4 (Notification to Report for Blood Testing) of the selection process had been overlooked. The military would not accept Tiny without completion of this step.

Told to report back to his local draft board, Tiny boarded the next bus back to Ashland, a distance of no more than 16 miles. After arriving in Ashland, Tiny confronted the local draft board the same day. He was told, "No problem. We have another group going the day after tomorrow. You'll go with them, and believe me, they'll take you, blood test or not!"

Two days later back in Huntington and somewhat apprehensive, Tiny saw the same man at the first desk. That time there was no question about blood testing. The man quickly waved Tiny on to the next station. After what seemed to be days standing in line, Tiny found himself being asked which branch of service he preferred. The fellow in front of Tiny, when asked said, "Navy." He went to the Army.

Reflecting on the advice of the baseball coach, Tiny replied with equal measures of reluctance and alarm, "I prefer the Army."

The man's response was immediate. He said, "No, Son, you are just ripe for the Navy, and you will be reporting to the Great Lakes Naval Training Station for training."

Tiny wished the coach could have seen the grin on his face as he went to be sworn in! Duard Vinson Gillum, Apprentice Seaman, Serial Number 828-63-79, all 107 pounds of him, proudly and with pleasure reported to Great Lakes, Illinois September 17, 1943. (Inductees were given a 7-day delay in departure.)

Originally, the spelling of Tiny's family's last name was "Gilliam". The boys spelled their last name that way when they started school, but later changed the spelling to "Gillum" because everyone emphasized the "i" when pronouncing the name when, in reality, the "i" was silent. With no birth certificates available, when the military sought birth records, they based the spelling of their last names on school records. Because of that, the brothers avoided any legal maneuvering in changing the spelling of their family name.

Upon arriving at Great Lakes, Tiny and the other inductees began the endless process of "lining up" for more medical examinations. This included shots for everything known to mankind and, in Tiny's case, the elusive blood test! General information gathering sessions, and issuance of clothing dominated the 1st day. What impressed Tiny the most was the fact that they received their first pay, a total of $5, that same day! Who could believe the Navy would pay a raw recruit on his 1st day?

The recruits did not have to wait long for an explanation of the 1st day's wages. At the first, each recruit was handed his bill. At each of the stalls following, they received an assortment of personal items such as toothpaste, razor, razor blades, shaving cream, shoe polish, and a bar of soap. At the last stall, a barber waited. After about six passes with his clippers up and over, he confiscated the $5 bill. The recruits appropriately referred to their first pay as "flying five."

After haircuts, the recruits were off to orientation lectures. At the orientation lectures various things such as insurance options, pay scales, basic boot camp rules, and service school opportunities were discussed. Selection for service school was based on civilian work experience and grades received on aptitude tests (yet to come). Following orientation, each boot was assigned to a specific company situated in one of several camps located at the training facility. At this time, the recruits retrieved the $5 bill given to them at the beginning! This is why Tiny believed his first Navy pay was appropriately called a "flying five!"

Approximately 130 recruits, including Tiny, were assigned to company 1417 in Camp Dewey. Half or more of the boots comprising this company hailed from Ashland. For the next 6 to 8 weeks, home for them would be a two-story dormitory which the men quickly learned was to be kept immaculate at all times.

As a means of instilling discipline, the men were introduced to "guard duty". They guarded the front and back door dormitory entrances, and even the laundry facilities (called the dryer) with 4-hour shifts. On one of those shifts, 2400 to 0400 (midnight to 4 a.m. civilian time) Tiny learned the meaning of military disciplinary action. While guarding the lower dormitory entrance, the front door guard challenged Tiny to hold reveille at 0100 (1 a.m.). Not one to let a challenge go unanswered, Tiny accepted the challenge, which he very soon regretted! He had to beat a hasty retreat when those sleepy eyed boots realized they had been tricked. That incident, reported to the company commander, netted Tiny one "happy hour", which proved not to be quite as happy as the name implied. With all gear, including sea bag and hammock, packed in what was termed "seagoing fashion", Tiny had to parade in front of the barracks without taking the gear from his shoulder except to change from one shoulder to the other. One tired prankster had learned his lesson, and there would be no more early reveilles called by Tiny.

The daily routine began at 0600 when the boots marched to the chow hall. Breakfast was followed by endless hours of arduous calisthenics, close order drills, obstacle courses, and abandon ship drills, pausing only for chow and an occasional 5-minute respite. The company commander commonly awakened the boots at 2400 hours and ordered them to fall out for a repeat of some portion of the day's activity that had not met his established expectations the first time around.

The boots looked forward to the weekends because, although, they were not permitted to leave the base on liberty, they were spared the rigors of the weekday training activities. After the rigorous training routines on weekdays, they were more than ready to just lie around the barracks, catch up on letter writing, read, play cards, or do absolutely nothing! One "must" requirement did exist on weekends. Everybody had to go to church Sunday mornings. With services for all denominations offered, they had no excuse not to attend.

On Saturday mornings they stood the captain's inspection, where personal appearance and living quarters had to be "up to snuff". One Saturday, returning from chow, one of Tiny's buddies playfully knocked Tiny's hat from his head. With the ground muddy from rain the night before, before Tiny could catch his hat, the hat hit the ground becoming slightly muddy on the back side. Since the mud was on the back side, Tiny thought nothing of what happened. When the captain began his revue, Tiny noticed the captain was removing approximately every 10th sailor's hat. He just knew he would be one of the unlucky ones. He was "right on"! When the captain removed Tiny's hat, he had no trouble seeing that little mud spot. Immediately he threw the hat to the ground, put his foot in the middle of the hat, and literally stomped the hat in the mud with all the delight he could display. He then looked Tiny straight in the eye, and said, "wash that hat, sailor!" After which he dealt Tiny some extra duty hours.

Boot camp ended November 9, 1943. The entire company, then Seamen 2nd Class, was granted a 9-day leave. Only about 10 or 12 members of the company were chosen to attend service as their next assignment. Tiny did not know then, or ever understand why he was one of the chosen few. Certainly not because of his formal education or civilian work experience because a junior high diploma would not have been sufficient for the qualification nor would his sheet metal, NYA, and other work experience have had anything to do with Tiny's selection for Quartermaster School.

"Quartermaster School," Tiny exclaimed! "I don't want to learn how to issue clothing and equipment!"

In response, Tiny was told that the duties of the U.S. Navy Quartermaster involved navigation, signaling, and helmsman duties. He still wasn't impressed! Tiny requested sea duty. However, with the powers to be in the driver's seat, Tiny's service school assignment remained in effect.

Returning to Ashland for his 9-day leave after being away only 2 months, Tiny found the sight of home surprisingly good. He secretly wished that he did not have to return to Great Lakes! Feeling important strutting up and down the streets of Ashland, Tiny enjoyed the attention from friends and relatives. His mom didn't want him out of his sight for a very long time. On occasion Tiny had to turn down invitations, which made Tiny feel uncomfortable. When the time came to return to Great Lakes, Tiny had mixed emotions. Not certain when, or if, he would return to Ashland, he felt a sense of finality that was hard to accept.

Tiny reported back to an Outgoing Unit (OGU) in Great Lakes for temporary assignment. There he awaited his transfer to Newport, Rhode Island where he would begin service school. Back at Great Lakes November 19, 1943, Tiny was assigned mess duty for the duration of his stay there. The main difference, other than the lack of training exercises, between OGU and boot camp was being able to get liberty a couple times each week. December 8 of the same year, Tiny shipped out to Newport, Rhode Island arriving there December 11 still not sold on the idea of service school.

The Newport Naval Base was located on Coddington Point on Narraganset Bay, an inlet extending into the state of Rhode Island. One of about 115 sailors comprising company 1586 of the 15th Quartermaster Battalion, Tiny discovered why he had been issued a hammock at Great Lakes. Bunks, cots, or any other "normal" sleeping accommodations were not available in the barracks. The sleeping area was equipped with a series of "hitching posts" to meet the needs of hanging hammocks. The sailors were issued spreader bars to insert in the hammocks to prevent their collapse. Learning to get into, stay in, and get out of one of those contraptions was not an experience too easily forgotten after returning from a beer drinking liberty!

Although the sailors shared a large living quarters, they were divided into smaller groups for classroom training. They arrived Saturday and commenced classes at 0800 sharp the following Monday. The instructor for Tiny's class was Frank S. Murray, Quartermaster 3rd Class. Tiny thought he must have had civilian teaching experience because he was very smooth; but did not appear to have been in the Navy long enough to have acquired such polished techniques.

The class covered two principle categories: navigation and visual signaling, which included "flag hoist", used to relay instructions for course changes, and other relevant information to other ships in a convoy by the arrangement of flags hoisted to the yardarm halyards. Tiny's interest in signaling increased in direct proportion to his decreasing interest in navigation!

As in civilian schools, graduation was not automatic. Four weeks into the curriculum, each sailor's progress was reviewed. At that time the decision was made as to whether the borderline students were worthy of continuance in the class.

Several factors were used to make that decision, interest and cooperation being major factors.

Tiny was very confident that he would be reassigned to different duties, thereby ending his school activities, which, of course, was his objective. Well, so much for Tiny's evaluation of others' opinions. His interview with this "wily" old chief and his instructor resulted in exactly the opposite!

The chief began by almost shouting, "Look, you little bastard, I know exactly what you are trying to 'pull off' here, and allow me to assure you it is not going to happen!" He continued, "You will remain in this class until it is over, so you might just as well 'wake up', and knock off this crap, because I am not known as one to reward the foolish who attempt to 'pull the wool over my eyes', so 'shape up, sailor!'"

Of course, Tiny thought the time for him to "shape up" was too late. He knew that he could never make up the time he had squandered early on.

Shortly after classes began, the sailors were granted an additional liberty, a Friday "overnighter". This was good and bad news! Although the extra time off base was welcomed, the sailors were under great pressure to get back to the base on time, change from their "tailor made" blues to Navy issue, and be ready to stand inspection at 0800 sharp. Most spent their weekend liberties in Newport or Providence, while Friday nights was reserved for Boston, Massachusetts, about 25 miles from Newport.

On Tiny's first "overnighter", he met a girl in Fall River, Massachusetts. She kept Tiny away from the evils of Boston!

At the end of one of Tiny's Friday night liberties, Tiny received his first extra duty at Newport. Arriving back to the base on time, Tiny made the necessary uniform change; but neglected to remove the white socks he had worn the night before, and replace them with regulation blue. Of course, by the time Tiny noticed his predicament, changing socks was out of the question, as he was already standing at attention as the inspection had already commenced. Tiny felt like the commanding officer must have been aware of his boo-boo. The officer immediately reached down and raised the right leg of Tiny's dress blues. That infraction cost Tiny 30 days restricted to the base.

Tiny got in trouble one other time while at Newport as a result of a Wednesday night liberty. Tiny and some of his buddies went to Newport for some beers. Next morning, with Tiny not quite ready for reveille, and failing to heed first call, the Master at Arms caught him sleeping.

The Master at Arms had a method of correction for such negligence. He always made a second pass through the Barracks, finding late risers and cutting the rope securing the foot of the sleeper's hammock. Later when Tiny went to the designated area for a new rope, he was assigned an extra 10 hours duty. Tiny knew better than to bypass the new rope issue! Another sailor had already tried that, only to be cut down on the first pass the next morning, and having his penalty doubled!

After Tiny's confrontation with the wily old chief and his instructor, Tiny's concentration on navigation was taken more seriously. However, failure to pay attention more seriously earlier had taken a toll, making understanding advanced techniques very difficult.

After 16 wild, but exciting weeks graduation time arrived April 3, 1944. Although Tiny's marks did not earn him a rate increase, the old chief taught Tiny a valuable lesson he never forgot: Once you start something, see it through to the end! Tiny finished only 1 point behind the class leader in visual signaling, but was somewhere close to the bottom of the ladder in navigation.

On April 5 just before leaving for Ashland on a 7-day leave, Tiny's instructor Quartermaster Murray presented him with a New Testament in which he had underlined Psalms 91:7, "A THOUSAND SHALL FALL AT THY SIDE, AND TEN THOUSAND AT THE RIGHT HAND, BUT IT SHALL NOT COME NIGH THEE." That was a gift that Tiny always treasured!

The old town had not changed much since Tiny was last there in November. Again, he was welcomed with open arms by relatives, friends, and strangers alike. Since leave time included travel, he could only spend 5 days at home.

After his short stay in Ashland, Tiny left for Little Creek, Virginia. His orders were to report at Little Creek April 15, a Saturday, for Amphibious Training. Immediately Tiny was assigned to Crew #7095; Landing Ship Medium (LSM); Group #420. For the next 6 weeks, they practiced amphibious landings operations daily. This included instructions for the offloading of invading troops and their supplies/fighting equipment in a safe and timely manner. Additionally, the group received training in firefighting, hand to hand combat, combat tactics, and defense against chemical warfare. They trained 5 days a week, leaving Saturday and Sunday free for liberty.

The closest town to Little Creek was Norfolk. One liberty trip to Norfolk was enough to convince Tiny the trip there had been 2 in 1...his first and his last! *What had transpired in the past to cause such poor relations between the city of Norfolk and the*

United States Navy, Tiny wandered? Telltale signs hung all over town, including many residences sporting signs reading "Dogs and Sailors, Keep off the Grass!" Most sailors, after spending one liberty there, called Norfolk "Shit City"!

Bootie, after completing boot camp at Great Lakes, was stationed at the naval air station near Norfolk. Visiting him at the air station was the only other time Tiny went near Norfolk. Other villages and towns nearby were more hospitable. Ocean City had a nice amusement park, which is where Tiny spent most of his nondrinking liberty time.

Although not as rough as boot camp, training at Little Creek left Tiny exhausted. The 72-hour pass he received at the end of his session was a welcome relief. Having been home twice in the last 6 months and because Baltimore was closer, Tiny opted to spend his liberty there. One of Tiny's buddies, Bobby Beisch, from Enterprise, Kansas joined him. They visited Bootie's wife Dorothy, their son Phil, and Tiny's mother, who had traveled from Ashland to spend time with Tiny. They also worked in some beer drinking at local bars. Once more, as in Ashland, people went overboard to make them welcome by buying them drinks. The trip was an overwhelming experience but all good things must end. Soon the two sailors were on their way back to Little Creek for further assignment.

The ship Tiny and his group was assigned to be on was being built by Brown Shipbuilding Company in Houston, Texas. They were transferred to Houston to await the ship's completion. They arrived there July 4, 1944 and were assigned temporary quarters at a nearby Army base, Camp Walters. The site at which they were temporarily housed also served as a holding area for German prisoners of war. After the prisoners were processed there, they were distributed to a variety of military installations in Texas, Louisiana, Oklahoma, and Arkansas for the duration of the war. Many of the prisoners later returned to the United States and became naturalized citizens, attesting to the manner in which America treated its prisoners...something that can hardly be said for any other nation in the world!

In a very short time, Tiny and his fellow sailors were notified that they had been assigned to LSM #36, which was ready to be commissioned. July 17, 1944 Tiny was honored to be asked to raise "Old Glory" on the ship for the first time. Many dignitaries were assembled on deck, as Tiny waited for the playing of the National Anthem (his signal to hoist the flag). Tiny's stomach was doing flip-flops. As the band began to play, Tiny prepared to raise the flag, which was previously attached to the halyard; but, in the excitement of the moment Tiny began pulling the hoist in the wrong direction, which would have caused the flag to be upside down. Fortunately, the flag was protected from view by a 3-foot high bulkhead circling the flag deck. Thus, Tiny only was aware of the error, and was able to reverse the direction of the flag before it came into view of those present on deck.

The ship was approximately 210 feet long and 33 feet wide. Bow doors opened up to a retractable ramp for loading and unloading both troops and equipment. The chart house and adjacent radio shack were located on the starboard superstructure deck, just aft of amidships. The conning tower, which contained the pilot house, towered high above the chart house. The flag deck was directly outside the pilot house. High atop the conning tower was the bridge.

LSM #36 Naval Ship Tiny Served on During WWII
Photo Retrieved 082618 from http://www.navsource.org/archives/10/14/14idx.htm

The normal compliment of an LSM was 52 enlisted men and four officers. Since Tiny's assigned ship was the flagship for LSM Group 5, they carried an additional 12 men and four officers. The extra crew was Group 5 staff responsible for directing and supporting the activities of the 12 ships in their group: USS LSMs 34-37, 130, 148-151, 205, and 314-315.

Lieutenant Commander Edward Gregory Smith, Jr. led Group 5. He was a salty old veteran who hailed from Old Lyme, Connecticut. Malcolm S. McLeod, a lieutenant from Calvin, North Dakota, served as skipper. Other officers included Lieutenant (jg) Jerome B. Harrison, executive officer and navigator; Ensign Frederick A. Sanford, communications officer; and, Ensign Elroy Utke, engineering officer. Of the 48 states then comprising the Union, 28 were represented aboard the ship.

Assigned to the bridge force, Tiny shared quartermaster duties with Michael Nutis, who was from Brooklyn, New York. In addition to Mike and Tiny, four others served in the group. Two sailors in the group were training to become signalmen, while two others aspired to be radiomen. With no chief petty officer in the bridge force, all personnel in that group reported directly to the communications officer.

The group was granted frequent liberties while in Galveston. Houston, approximately 40 miles away, was another popular attraction for the sailors. Both cities offered many attractions to allure a sailor on liberty. Tiny's liberty privileges ended soon after he and his signalman buddy Maynard L. Jones celebrated Tiny's 19th birthday at Galveston's Congo Club! Arriving aboard ship just as the breakfast chow line was forming, the two sailors hopped into line. The chief boatswain, a man with no love for any of the bridge force personnel, ordered Jones and Tiny to "grab a broom, and chase it around the deck."

Tiny told him to have one of his "deck apes" chase his broom. What a poor choice of words on Tiny's part!

The officer let Tiny know that as long as he wore a white hat, he would do as told, whether he was a member of his deck force, or not! Tiny's next remark likewise had no calming effect. He volunteered to go below and come back wearing a blue hat. Tiny outran the officer to avoid physical injury; but, the officer put Tiny on report.

The officer's report resulted in a captain's mast for insubordination to a chief petty officer and netted Tiny 30 hours extra duty, plus 30 days restriction to the ship. Just to round out the situation, Tiny's extra duties were to be administered by the chief! Since they were already under orders to set sail for the Pacific theater of operations in 4 weeks, Tiny would not have seen too many more liberties anyway. Time was spent attending to last minute details before heading out to sea, including a 3-day "shakedown cruise" in the Gulf of Mexico. Shakedowns were intended to test equipment and systems, as well as the sea legs of an inexperienced crew. The Gulf of Mexico can be rough at times. That was one of those times! A first experience with sea sickness convinced Tiny (and others) if that was anything like what was to come, they were in deep trouble.

Once back in safe harbor, everyone continued with the work of completing tasks in preparation for their impending journey. Mike and Tiny kept busy updating charts they would be using, and brushing up on the navigation techniques soon to be applied for the first time under actual sailing conditions. Mike had obviously been more attentive in service school than Tiny had been. Thus, Mike really had a knack for getting Tiny's attention. Tiny learned more from Mike in a very short time than he did in the entire 16 weeks of service school. The one-on-one teaching and "hands on" experience by far exceeded what Tiny had gained in the classroom.

The duties of quartermaster aboard their ship proved advantageous for Mike and Tiny. Part of their job was to plot the course to destinations, which enabled them to receive a copy of the orders before an announcement was made to the crew. Their first orders were: "DEPART GALVESTON ON THURSDAY, AUGUST 31, 1944, AT 0800 HOURS; PROCEED TO COLON" (a seaport at the Caribbean end of the Panama Canal). Suddenly Mike and Tiny were the most popular sailors aboard ship. Everyone wanted to know where they were going; but, of course, the two quartermasters could not say anything.

The captain revealed the destination to the crew a few days prior to sailing, relieving everyone's anxiety. On Wednesday, August 30 members of the crew eligible for liberty (which did not include Tiny) scurried down the gangplank for a last night on shore in the United States. Busying himself in the chart house, Tiny was surprised by a visit from Ensign Sanford, who asked, "How would you like to go on liberty?" With a resounding affirmative reply from Tiny, he continued, "I'm lifting your restriction, so get your ass ashore, and you had better be back on time."

Soon Jonesy and Tiny were on their way to Houston, where they found plenty to do and plenty to drink. However, their timing was not the best. They were having such a good time; they missed the last shuttle back to the ship. They started walking and trying to hitch a ride. They walked most of the way arriving at the ship about 0730, one half hour prior to the scheduled departure. Had Jonesy and Tiny been 5 minutes later, they would have missed the ship. For reasons known only to him, the captain decided to cast off early. This forced the two sailors to leap aboard as all lines were being hauled in. They barely got on the ship in time before they were off to war in the South Pacific.

***

CHAPTER 4

World War II...Sea Duty

After scrambling aboard ship at 0730 with Tiny scheduled for the 0800-1200 watch, he made a mad dash to change and get to the bridge! Ensign Sanford displayed considerable relief, perhaps thinking Tiny had really "missed the boat", which would have put him in a very compromising position if (as Tiny suspected) he had lifted Tiny's restriction without the skipper's approval. With the ship hardly out of Galveston Bay, they ran into bad weather and heavy seas. Seasickness hit Tiny early and stayed late...all the way to Colon, 9 days later. Tiny savored sack time; but, with his portion of the signal watch and quartermaster duties to perform, he had little time for extra sleep.

Tiny carried a trusty "bucket" with him from bridge to bunk and bunk to bridge around the clock hoping he would die and afraid he might not. Although, Tiny was not alone. The captain was not seen "topside" for several days. Mike and Tiny were on the superstructure deck outside the chart house, practicing their sextant skills, when he finally made his first appearance since leaving Galveston. The first words out of his mouth were, "What's that peculiar smell?"

World War II...Sea Duty

"It could be fresh air, Captain," Mike retorted very quickly.

The ship reached Colon September 8 but due to heavy volume traffic waiting to enter the Panama Canal, the port director advised them they would have to stand by overnight. The Panama Canal at that point in time was a lot like California freeways today!

Once in port the sailors found many of the narrow streets of Colon lined with houses of "ill repute", above which businesses operated (mostly bars, of course). Jonesy and Tiny made their way along the main street of town, thinking they would find a place where they might enjoy a couple of cold beers. Sightseeing was out of the question. Even walking the streets was a hazard; due to the amount of prostitutes trying to solicit business...they literally grabbed men by the arm, and tried to drag them inside! In time, Jonesy and Tiny found what they hoped would be the haven they sought. No sooner had they made their way upstairs to a bar, before they even had a chance to order, a fight between two sailors and three or four Panamanians broke out.

The police must have been at the foot of the stairs waiting for a fight to happen, judging by the speed in which they were on the scene. The sailors escaped by jumping from the balcony, but the Panamanians were not so lucky...and those cops were mean! Before hustling their prisoners off to jail, they administered a sound beating to each of them. This would assure there would be no further attempts at escape. As soon as calm was restored, Jonesy and Tiny made a hasty retreat back to the security and comfort of their ship. They cut their liberty short by several hours, voluntarily.

Early next morning, September 9, the sailors began their trip through the canal, a distance of about 50 miles. Due to the heavy traffic, many delays occurred. They did not complete the journey through the canal until 2 days later. Once out on the Pacific side, they set a southwesterly course on their way to Bora-Bora in the Society Islands.

THE DOMAIN OF NEPTUNUS REX

Crossing the equator for the first time is an event no sailor can forget. Their initiation came September 17 with all the traditional ceremonies and rituals. Those aboard who had been previously initiated were "in charge". They took great delight in the administration of events honoring the occasion!

One thing that stood out vividly in Tiny's mind was being blindfolded and led around a table, while being told of the mixture of which every man would be required to partake. Each of the sailors being initiated were told the mixture consisted of blood, sweat, spit, and snot; every "mother's son" would have to eat; and, failure to do so willingly would, naturally, result in the mixture being forced down one's throat. One by one, they were forced to swallow a spoonful of what was, in reality, raw egg. Some of the sailors could not deal with the raw egg and actually vomited, which led to some hard feelings, which passed quickly enough though. Order was soon restored. Following the ceremony, each of the inductees was given a card proclaiming them to be "A Trusty Shellback" in the Domain of Neptunus Rex.

Seventeen days after emerging from the Panama Canal, the sailors docked at Bora-Bora. All the seasickness and discomforts were forgotten quickly. They had, indeed, reached "the" south sea island of every man's dreams. Native women of incredible beauty with golden tans and skin that looked like silk were everywhere the sailors looked. They were told to only look (and not too hard) and never touch under any circumstances! Reports existed that the local men did not take too kindly to strangers gawking at their lovely lassies and that to do so would result in trouble.

While on shore Tiny bought a stalk of bananas for the princely sum of $1 because fresh fruit was such a rarity aboard ship. Bananas were then, and remained a favorite food of Tiny's! Of course, Tiny shared the bananas with others aboard the ship! After a few days in Bora-Bora, the sailors were underway for Espiritu Santo in the New Hebrides Islands.

THE DOMAIN OF THE IMPERIAL DRAGON

October 4 the sailors crossed the 180th Meridian (International Date Line) and "lost" a day! This would be a temporary loss because; on their way back they would gain the day back. Hopefully that would not be too long! When one crosses this line of demarcation for the first time he becomes a member of "The Domain of the Imperial Dragon" by tradition. This milestone is somewhat less important than crossing the Equator; therefore, no special rituals were performed. Nevertheless, in no more than 2 weeks, they had been made a part of two of the Navy's prestigious orders!

October 10, 1944 the ships reached Espiritu Santo. The sailors spent 6 days taking on supplies and fuel for the remainder of their journey. While there they had a beer party on the beach; but, other than that, there was not much for which to go ashore. The biggest surprise on this spit of land in such a vast sea was a large Coca-Cola bottling company! Judging by the size of the company, they must have supplied Coke for the entire South Pacific.

While at Espiritu Santo the sailors were rewarded with a very welcome personnel change (at least to Tiny!). The chief boatswain with whom Tiny had the altercation with at Galveston, resulting in his restriction to the ship, was replaced by Chief Boatswain Frank H. Hill of Saint Louis, Missouri. Diametrically different from the chief being replaced, Chief Hill operated with calm and dignity. Instead of relying on authority and with contempt for the men under his control, he treated every man as a gentleman. He won both our respect and total cooperation, which resulted in greatly improved relations between the deck force, bridge force, and the engineering group.

While reviewing personnel records, Chief Hill discovered Tiny's extra duty hours were still "on the books". Everyone had been so busy since leaving the States; there had been no time for working off any such extra duty hours. To the replaced chief's credit, he had not forced the issue in Tiny's case. Chief Hill scheduled a meeting with Tiny. After hearing the circumstances leading up to the extra duty hours, the new chief seemed displeased with his predecessor's handling of the issue. He scheduled a series of meetings between himself and Tiny, whereby the extra duty hours were eliminated one by one. Later Chief Hill was very instrumental in Tiny's promotion to Seaman 1st Class.

After Espiritu Santo the sailors spent 6 days at sea headed for the island of Manus, located in the Admiralty group of islands, a part of the Bismarck Archipelago. They arrived there October 22. The

World War II...Sea Duty

ships remained at Manus for 6 days while the sailors took on supplies and fuel. By this time the stock of fresh foods, which was never too great, had been exhausted. They had been forced to rely on those "delicious" dehydrated foods...potatoes, milk, eggs, and canned meats, notably Spam! All the flour had long since been contaminated by weevils; but, only the white flour was a problem. Since the presence of weevils was not apparent in the wheat flour, no one knew it or worried about it.

At Manus another personnel change occurred. The Navigator and Executive Officer Mister Harrison, was transferred from the 36 to new duties elsewhere. Although in time, he was replaced, the replacing officer had little experience in navigation. This, however, did not pose a problem. Normally, navigation is not the primary task of a ship's quartermaster. This was not the case on board the 36. For whatever reason, Mike and Tiny assumed these responsibilities shortly after departing Galveston and remained in that role the entire time they were aboard.

Not only did Mike and Tiny perform the navigation duties for the 36, on more than one occasion Lieutenant Commander Smith utilized our skills for Group 5 activities. By this time due to Mike's fine tutorage, Tiny had become more proficient in navigation. This allowed them to alternate the navigation responsibilities on a daily basis. Of course, in addition to their navigation obligations, they had their portion of the signal watch to perform. The signal watch was divided into 4 segments (i.e.: 0400-0800, 0800-1200, etc.). The watch schedule was on a four man rotation basis consisting of Signalmen Maynard Jones and Albert Humrich, in addition to Mike and Tiny.

Since Mike and Tiny were on watch 4 hours and then off for 12 hours, they had some most welcomed free time. Most of this time they spent devoted to writing letters, reading, and catching up on their chart corrections task. This was something that seemed to never end!

Since chart corrections were not near as urgent as the other navigational duties, chart correction were put on the back burner most times, which quite often resulted in a very heavy backlog. Fortunately, Mike and Tiny had some additional assistance in the chart corrections task. Rufus Sizemore, a seaman who was a quartermaster striker, was assigned to their area. A navy striker is someone who is performing duties in a certain specialty to qualify for a petty officer rating in that particular specialty.

Seaman Sizemore was a very ambitious young man who was willing to learn, never complained, and was always very thorough in the performance of his assigned duties. Due to his efforts, the free time Mike and Tiny had did not need to be entirely spent on official duties, which pleased them a lot.

On October 29 the ships got underway for Hollandia, New Guinea, which would become their base of operations for what was termed "milk runs" (routine, insignificant) deploying troops and equipment. What Tiny remembered most about New Guinea was the torrential rains that occurred there. He had never seen rains like that before in his life. The rain was hard enough and steady enough that Tiny was afraid to step outside the chart house in fear of being drowned!

In Hollandia, the sailors experienced their first so-called "air raid" by a lone Japanese bomber. The bomber flew over the island about midnight...he did this every night they were told…doing little more than disturbing what might, otherwise, have been a full night's sleep. Circling around, he was never known to have dropped a bomb, thus earning the name "Piss Call Charlie". In Hollandia 6 nights, the sailors never missed a call!

Tiny remembered one of their so called "milk runs" to the island of Morotai in the Netherlands East Indies. They were there 3 nights. Each night the Japanese conducted an air raid. Although these raids were of more significance than the "Piss Call Charlie" sessions, the raids could not be classified as major events. Commencing November 15 and ending November 19, they took part in two invasions, the first for LSM Group Five. To Tiny, the islands of Mapia and Asia, located east of Morotai, did not seem to be of any significant importance. However, someone somewhere thought the islands were important enough to warrant their attention. The Americans landed on both beaches under cover of darkness with a minimum amount of resistance, which was most welcome!

After the invasion of Mapia and Asia, they set sail for Hollandia, with a short stopover at Biak and Numfor, islands off the coast of New Guinea. From there, they moved on to Hollandia where they, once more, replenished some of their food supplies. Then they set sail for Sansapor, New Guinea, where they were to prepare for their biggest and most important invasion of WWII.

Among their duties as quartermaster, Mike and Tiny were required to prepare daily reports, alternating in presenting them to the skipper at 1200 hours each and every day. Minimally, the reports contained their current location, the course they were following (if underway), speed, weather conditions, and, most important to the captain, notification that the chronometers had been wound. From the outset, Mike had insisted Tiny and he present more than the minimum, which pleased the captain immensely.

Arriving in Sansapor December 15, that day Mike instructed Tiny to present only the minimum when delivering the skipper's daily report. When Tiny questioned him as to why, Mike insisted he do as he said. After Tiny finished the report, the captain asked, "Is that all?"

"Yes, Sir," Tiny replied.

The captain promptly dismissed Tiny; but, as Tiny left the wardroom, he noticed a puzzled look on the captain's face that he never forgot.

The next day Mike followed his own advice in preparing only the minimum for the daily report to be given to the captain. The captain again asked, "Is that all?"

"No, sir," Mike responded. "I think Gillum and I both deserve promotions, Sir!"

Shortly thereafter, Tiny received his Quartermaster 3rd Class strip while Mike received a promotion to 2nd Class. Suddenly Tiny realized not only was Mike a fine quartermaster; he was some kind of a politician.

Tiny's second navy Christmas was spent in Sansapor. Four days later the Japanese delivered a belated Christmas present! The present was in the form of an air raid considerably more intense than those of "Piss Call Charlie". However, no damages incurred. On December 30 LSM Group Five departed Sansapor for rendezvous with Flotilla Two, a convoy of about 300 ships of all types. Under heavy air cover, the convoy proceeded in a northwesterly direction past the Philippine Islands of Mindanao, Leyte, and

Mindoro, then north to Lingayen Gulf in the northwest part of Luzon. Along the way Japan mounted several attacks using midget two man submarines and suicide aircraft and boats. They did not encounter any major naval forces because the enemy's navy had been somewhat neutralized during the Battle of the Coral Sea. Tokyo Rose, the propaganda voice of Japan, issued repeated warnings that the Japanese Air Force was "ready and waiting for us". The warnings proved to be accurate!

As the Ally ships approached the entrance to Manila Bay, all "hell" broke loose. The Japanese darkened the sky with fighter planes (Zeros), but they were no match for the Allies superior firepower. The fighter planes quickly repelled. One of their pilots intentionally ditched in the sea and was picked up by one of the ships in the convoy. The pilot revealed in English that he had attended school in the United States and had returned to Japan a short time before the bombing of Pearl Harbor. Not then being allowed to leave Japan, he joined the suicide squadron with full intention of deserting at the first opportunity. He related how, dressed in white, his funeral service had been conducted prior to his mission of death.

Suicide pilots were taught the art of becoming airborne but given no instructions whatsoever (according to the deserting pilot) on landing procedures. Their superiors were very fearful they might land in enemy territory, if they knew how!

Tokyo Rose was a sexy talking woman who filled the airwaves with enemy propaganda and played the latest American music. She did this to get and keep our attention while she taunted us with, "I had mine last night, did you get yours?" or "Hey Joe, what do you think your wife (or girlfriend) is doing right now? Surely you don't think she stays home every night!"

The American sailors accepted Tokyo Rose's garbage as the price they had to pay for enjoying the very best, most popular, good old American music, with which she was abundantly stocked. The sailors continued to listen to Tokyo Rose's music (if not her B.S.) night after night as they maintained their course for Lingayen Gulf, and what would prove to be a very exciting experience.

The softening-up bombardment began in the pre-dawn darkness Tuesday, January 9, 1945, and would soon be followed by troops storming ashore. At that time, the fight would belong to the on-land American troops. Until the Navy landed the troops safely on the beach, the battle belonged to the Navy.

Enemy fire from shore batteries was intense, as well as their air cover. What one sees in the movies is far from what one feels under the actual circumstances. Tiny had no description of the feeling that gripped his mind and body. Although there were ships everywhere Tiny looked, he had the feeling that his ship was the only one the enemy could see and that all the enemy devices were aimed straight at him. People who have never experienced this may think you only have to head for the nearest piece of shore, dump your load, and "haul ass" out of there. Sadly, the situation wasn't that simple! Every ship had a specified area of beach on which that ship must land the troops. Otherwise, the manpower and material, so vital to the operation, might not be anywhere close to where they were needed.

The battle plan of every offensive action takes such logistics into account. Every group and every ship in each group must be responsible to perform their assigned duty. In truth, when you begin the run, you have a target area to hit. The success of the mission, in large part, depends on everyone doing his job efficiently and as ordered. That is why discipline is terribly important in the world of the military. Knowing that the young men huddled there knowing that some, if not all, may never see another sunrise and that your task is to deliver them to their fate can be a sobering thought; one that lets you focus on something other than your own life and concern for your safety. But, there's a job to do, so you put the danger out of your mind and do what has to be done.

LSM 36 was equipped with a large ramp that thrusted forward as the bow doors swung open, then dropped at the bow of the ship, allowing soldiers and material to be unloaded quickly. The longer the ship sits there waiting to be emptied, the less chance of making another trip. Shore batteries, given the opportunity to get off as few as three rounds, can obliterate a ship such as an LSM. If a howitzer crew can see you, they can destroy you. Sometimes they fire one round over or beyond a target followed by another round under or short of the target to effectively establish range. Then they "fire one for effect". By then, if you are still sitting on the beach, you may sit there forever! Fortunately, for Tiny's group, the Japanese had established their principal firepower to cover what they believed were more strategic locations than those to which they were assigned. Although they encountered considerable enemy fire both during the approach to the beach and while on the beach, luck prevailed. Soon they were hauling up the ramp and reversing engines to get out of harms' way before any serious damage could be inflicted on them.

The next assignment of the Navy was to ferry ammunition to the shore. Ammunition supply ships, standing offshore beyond shore abased artillery range, were totally dependent on air cover, together with whatever protection other ships in the fleet could provide. Even so, taking on a load tethered to an ammunition ship can make a man nervous. Surprisingly, Tiny thought everything was going pretty well. At this time, he and Ensign Sanford had the watch. When Tiny commented on how smoothly things were going...thinking, perhaps, the battle was all over but the shouting, Sanford brought Tiny out of his reverie, and said, "Just when things are going well, something invariably goes wrong."

The ensign's words were still echoing when they heard the roar of a Kamikaze coming directly out of the sun. As he was making his dive toward them, the pilot saw other what he probably thought was better game elsewhere. As he leveled off though, he dropped a bomb that hit a small boat tied up to the other side of the ammunitions ship that they were offloading. Then, they were told later, the pilot flew headlong into a battleship anchored a short distance away. As the pilot crossed their fantail, they could actually see the big grin on his face. Needless to say, Tiny found that experience very scary!

Neither LSM 36 nor the ammunition ship was damaged. However, one young sailor in the small boat alongside lost his life, all within minutes after Tiny's boast of how well things were going. Another report received was that a high ranking officer on the battleship also was killed. Many times over the years Tiny later thought how much worse the situation could have been that January morning. He thanked God for His protection that day and many more days that would follow in similar circumstances.

For 3 days after the initial landings, the LSM 36 shuttled back and forth from supply ships to the beach, ferrying ammunition and supplies. Their air cover was superb, as was the support they received from their Navy buddies. They maintained a constant barrage of fire to keep the enemy off their backs. Without all of them, the situation might have ended much more different.

The Japanese made every effort they could to penetrate America's defenses. In addition to Kamikazes, they even used two-man suicide submarines! Loaded with explosives, these little subs had only one purpose in life...to sneak under and behind our protection, to ram a ship. Any ship would do; the bigger, the better. But, when you stop to think about the situation, why should they be particular? Their funeral services back home had already been conducted. The Japanese Emperor had already decorated them for bravery in the service. All these men had to do was blow themselves up in the belly of some ship, any ship would do, even a little old LSM. This certainly kept the American sailors on their guard 24 hours a day, as if they didn't already have enough to worry about. This was not the only trick of the Japanese.

Consider the following trick: individual Japanese would station himself somewhere along the beach well hidden from view only armed with a knife and a box. Under cover of darkness with the wooden box over his head, he would swim slowly and silently toward a ship looking to the unsuspecting like a bit of flotsam drifting. When the individual Japanese thought circumstances were safe for him to do so, he would board a ship hoping to make his way to the crew's quarter's and slash as many throats as possible before being discovered. In defense, the American Navy officers assigned an extra man to every gun crew on every watch. The extra man was stationed on the bridge and had orders to fire on anything that even "might" be an attack on the 36. Although, reassuring to have a rifleman with an itchy trigger finger at Tiny's side during his watch, the situation created a hardship on the crew. A ship, any ship, has a complement of men, each assigned to duties. With the naval commanders having to assign such extra duty put a strain on crewmen that might have otherwise been able to do other things (rest, hopefully).

On January 12, accompanied by destroyers and destroyer escorts, the 36 got underway for Leyte in the Southern Philippines. The trip took about 5 days. They encountered little enemy resistance. By then, the American Navy had gained control of the seas in that area. Any resistance encountered was minimal and short-lived.

At Leyte, from January 17-27, they enjoyed a brief respite, after which they headed for Mindoro, and more "milk runs". From January to April, the sailors on 36 were like spit on a griddle. The commanding officers kept them hopping from island to island, relocating troops and equipment and providing support for several invasions like Lubang, Zamboanga, and the city of Davao in Mindanao; none of which approached the intensity of the Lingayen Gulf operations, but they did have their moments.

Upon arrival at Lubang, the sailors tied the 36 up to a floating concrete pier left behind by the enemy. Although they had been informed the pier had been mined, they had no concern for the safety of the ship and crew because they also were told the mine had no detonator, so was "harmless". While there, the crew was notified that several Japanese suicide boats had been located in a nearby lagoon. The skipper of the 36 requested, and was granted, permission to lead a group of volunteers on a mission to seize one or more of these vessels for later use as Liberty boats. This was the opportunity Tiny had been waiting for! Remember, he went into the navy thinking, naively, he would become a hero, and now was his chance. Tiny learned otherwise quickly!

Stealthily approaching the lagoon on foot, via a winding dirt trail, the skipper suddenly grabbed Tiny by the arm and pulled him off the path. There, in the middle of the trail about where Tiny's next step would have fallen was a piece of bamboo about 10 inches long, hollowed out and filled with explosives. Without the captain's observance and quick action, this tale might never have been written or, if so, with a totally different ending. Never the less, Tiny's volunteering days came to an abrupt end right then and there.

The bow end of each Japanese suicide boat was packed solid with explosives. A depth charge was attached to each end of a rope secured across the bow. As these boats neared their targets, the operator was expected to cut the rope securing the depth charges allowing them to sink and explode when they reached their pre-set depth. Because the boat had no reverse gear, once near enough to his target to release the charges, the operator had no time to change course. He was expected to continue at full speed and ram the target.

The volunteers from the 36 floated three of the boats back to the ship. Keeping one for their own use, the other two boats were made available to other ships in their group. After removing the explosives, the engineering group modified the engine and added a reverse gear, making a pretty good Liberty boat.

Back aboard the ship the captain gave the order to cast off from the concrete pier and they were on their way congratulating themselves on such cleverness. About 400 or 500 yards from the pier to which they had been tied until minutes before, an enormous explosion destroyed the pier! The pier may not have had a detonator, but something sure caused the pier to blow. Perhaps there was an internal device scheduled to go off at that pre-set time. Whatever, another 90 seconds at that pier would have been disastrous for the 36 and her crew.

On May 9, the 36 and her crew resumed "milk run" duty throughout the Philippines and the Sulu Archipelago. After a short period, they began preparation for the invasion of Borneo, which would be their 10th and, as it turned out, the last invasion of World War II. The 36 and her crew spent approximately 3 weeks in Morotai preparing for the trip to Balikpapan on the southeast coast of Borneo.

Setting sail from Morotai June 26, the 36 reached Borneo July 1. As in the Lingayen Gulf operations, intense air and naval bombardment preceded amphibious landings. The 36 crew made several trips to the beach after an initial discharge of soldiers and equipment, before proceeding to anchor offshore.

Borneo was a great oil producer. Several oil wells were set ablaze by the relentless bombing and shelling. For the anchorage of the 36 offshore, they could see the flames from fires; several located not too far inland. The flames, 100's of feet into the air, must have been visible for many, many miles. A United States B-24 bomber was shot down by the Japanese shore batteries during this action. The crew bailed out, but the pilot stayed aboard, and glided his dead aircraft into the sea about 50 yards off the port bow of 36. Rescue boats responded quickly. The pilot was plucked from the sea as his plane went under. All this transpired in what seemed to Tiny to be a very few minutes. The vantage point of 36 had to be abandoned. Soon after dropping anchor and securing battle stations, Japanese mortar fire began landing much too close for comfort. With a big ocean, they simply weighed anchor, and moved out of range.

The 36 departed Balikpapan July 2 destined for Morotai to pick up replacement troops for the Borneo operation. When they returned 2 weeks later, the oil wells were still burning and showed no sign of diminishing. By this time, Americans had firmly established the beachhead. Only mop-up operations remained to be completed. Most of the enemy had been killed or captured. Of those still in fighting condition, most had fled inland and probably fell victim to Borneo's cannibal population.

Completing the mission to Borneo, the crew of 36 was ordered to Leyte where they were to enter dry dock for some much needed overhaul and repair. There Tiny celebrated his 20th birthday! Unlike his 19th birthday celebrated the previous year in Galveston, Tiny celebrated this birthday with nothing more than a few beers with his buddies.

When the crew heard the news of the bombing of Hiroshima, Japan August 6, they knew the war would soon be over. Descriptions of the damage inflicted by that first ever dropped Atom bomb were incredible…something no one had witnessed in the history of warfare. Three days later, when the city of Nagasaki was hit, they really knew.

August 14, 1945, officially V - J Day was an anticlimax. The crew of 36 received word August 10 of Japan's agreement to unconditional surrender. Tiny never forgot that day. He was standing anchor watch. The skipper had given him permission to attend the movie being shown on the well deck. Being able to see a movie was a treat for Tiny. Little did he know what was on the horizon!

The captain had given Tiny orders to occasionally check the anchorage position for possible drifting. During one of those safety checks, as Tiny ascended the ladder to the bridge, three red flares lit up the sky. This being the established signal for air raid alert, Tiny headed straight for the bridge, and sounded General Quarters. Festivities on deck stopped immediately, as all hands rushed to their assigned battle stations. After a brief lapse, allowing everyone to reach battle stations, the message came via the ship's radio…THE WAR IS OVER! Since there was no pre-arranged "end of the war" signal, the air raid warning was the quickest way to get everyone's attention.

The captain passed the word to break out the beer and the long-awaited celebration was underway. Surrender had come none too soon for the crew of 36. They already had orders and courses had been plotted for the invasion of Honshu, Japan's southernmost and largest island. With peace at hand, the common word was "let's go home", but such was not the fate of the crew of 36.

The ship entered dry dock as planned for the scheduled overhaul and repair. At this time, Mike and Tiny reverted to their previous practice of presenting only the minimum with the noon report. As before, their actions worked. Mike moved up to 1st Class. Tiny exchanged his 3rd Class stripes for 2nd Class. They remained in dry dock for several days, during which vital repairs on the ship were completed. Meanwhile, Mike and Tiny busied themselves plotting courses and making chart corrections that had been postponed during the Borneo invasion and subsequent "milk run" duty. The cry to "go home" intensified among crew members, though good-natured grousing, since they knew they'd be going home in a matter of time. Repairs completed, the 36 began transporting troops to Jinsen (now known as Inchon) and Fusan (now Pusan), Korea. After the first trip to Korea, we sailed to Manila (capital of Luzon) where they picked up more troops and supplies to be taken to Jinsen.

On October 7, the 36 encountered a large scale typhoon in the China Sea. Winds were so fierce they had to lash heavy manila lines to all outside ladders and walkways for support, and to keep personnel from being washed overboard. Swells were so high they crashed over the ship's bow, putting them under water for brief periods. They could make no headway! All ships in Group 5 were ordered to cut all engines, conserve fuel, and ride out the storm.

After about 3 days, the winds subsided and the crew of 36 was able to make their way to Okinawa, minus their bow doors which had been ripped away by the rough seas. As they entered Okinawa's Buckner Bay, damage there revealed they too had felt the wrath of the typhoon. The crew of 36 saw large Liberty ships high and dry on the beach. Many small boats had been destroyed; some of which were resting in the tops of trees. Requesting docking instructions from the port director's tower, Tiny also inquired as to the damage inflicted by the typhoon. They flashed back: E-V-E-R-Y-T-H-I-N-G D-E-S-T-R-O-Y-E-D B-U-T P-O-R-T D-I-R-E-C-T-O-R S-T-O-W-E-R! In other words, "You're on your own, and good luck."

The crew of 36 was able to muster up some fuel and continue their journey to Manila. Their first visit to Manila being somewhat brief and under different circumstances, none of them had gone ashore to see the sights. This time circumstances were different. Most of the crew went aboard two or more times. Manila was the largest town they had seen since leaving the States. Manila's many night clubs and restaurants were something the sailors had looked forward to for some time.

The sailors were warned to visit Manila with caution because mean looking armed Guerrillas roamed the streets there. Not only were the Guerrillas mean looking, they were mean making the local police force (which was hardly polite society) look like a pack of cub scouts!

One night Jonesy and Tiny were having a few beers in a joint that featured a small dance band. A young lady (?) asked Tiny to dance. Although not overly fond of dancing, Tiny decided to give it a whirl. However, before accepting her invitation, he consulted her Guerrilla escort, asking whether he could dance with her. He said, "Sure, Joe."

As soon as the girl and Tiny reached the dance floor, Tiny's Guerrilla "friend" hauled out a pistol, aiming in their direction! Jonesy shouted a warning. Tiny dropped to the floor pulling the girl down with him. They then crawled to their table from which Jonesy and Tiny made their way to the back door exiting to the safety of darkness outside. They heard shots as they rushed to escape, but heard nothing to indicate any one had been hit…and never bothered to inquire.

October 20, 1945
At Manila, Philippine Islands

With new bow doors in place, the 36 was ready to sail. They departed Manila October 31 for Jinsen via Lingayen Gulf, where they were to pick up troops who were joining the occupation forces in Korea. Out of Lingayen, they hit choppy seas that made walking a little hazardous, but nothing compared to typhoon conditions.

One of the soldiers we were transporting, firmly planted against an army vehicle, saw one of the 36 crew members near the lifeline. Thinking the seaman was sick, the soldier said, "What's the matter buddy, too rough for you?"

The seaman quickly retorted, "No, it doesn't get rough until the ship starts leaping from wave to wave."

During a tropical storm the next day, the same inquiring soldier was seen bent over the lifeline "feeding the fish". The seaman could not resist the temptation to tap the soldier on the back and ask, what's the matter soldier, too rough for you?"

Fortunately, the storm was of short duration allowing the 36 to arrive in Jinsen as scheduled, November 14. The next day, November 15, they were ordered to depart for Saishu To, a small island off the southern tip of Korea. The crew of the 36 went there expecting to evacuate a group of Japanese soldiers that had occupied the island. This assignment caused concern because the sailors had never before transported enemy troops. *What if*, the sailors wondered, *they don't know the war is over? What would be their reaction to us?* To the sailors' relief, what they found there were only local citizens and military vehicles. They loaded the vehicles and returned to Jinsen never knowing what happened to the troops, which they lost no sleep over.

Jensen's harbor had no breakwater with heavy waves very common. The crew experienced the highest tide conditions there than in any other port they visited. On their first landing there in September, crew members faced a new experience. Under normal conditions, amphibious landings are made at high tide to allow ample time for unloading and retraction from the beach. Remember, an LSM

World War II...Sea Duty

actually deposits its cargo on the beach, or as close to the beach as possible, depending on the depth of the water in that particular area. The landing in September began as normal but when they had completed unloading, the skipper gave no retraction order. After a time, Tiny reminded him that low tide was due in about 4 hours.

The captain replied, "Very well, Gillum."

Three hours later Tiny reminded the captain once more. Pointing out that low tide would be upon them in no more than an hour. He retorted, "Very well, Gillum, and thank you!"

Puzzled by the skipper's diffidence, Tiny hesitated to make further announcements and waited further instructions. Soon the ship was high and dry on the beach! Then, with all the subtly of a whale in a minnow farm, the captain picked up his hand held speaker and said, "Now hear this, all hands turn to and scrape and paint the ship below the waterline!"

By the time the next high tide arrived, the ship below the waterline had been scraped and painted. Tiny never again had to remind the skipper of tides or times!

The crew of 36 spent Thanksgiving, 1945 in Jinsen celebrating the occasion by partaking in a traditional Thanksgiving dinner, complete with frozen turkey! Tiny didn't remember where the turkey came from; but, reported the meat was quite an improvement over Spam!

SNOW soon arrived! The morning of December 1 dawned with snow falling, the first Tiny had seen in 2 years. The snowfall continued for 2 or 3 days. Mixed with hail, the sailors did not find the snow a treat, but gave them more than enough motivation to move out. On December 4, the sailors were happy to set sail for Saipan in the Mariana Islands. Their orders were to proceed to Saipan via Guam and to go through a screening process once in Saipan to determine which crew members would be eligible for immediate discharge on arrival in the United States. At least, the sailors knew someone was thinking about home other than themselves!

At war's end the military high command at the Pentagon (presumably) devised a "point" system by which eligibility for discharge or rotation would be determined. The system was based on age, time in service, months of combat and/or foreign service, plus decorations (if any) for valorous conduct. A total of 80 points qualified a man for immediate rotation to the States and discharge. With enough points accumulated, Tiny found the screening process unchallenging. However, at Guam the sailors learned that their screening process in Saipan had been cancelled. They were ordered to proceed directly to the United States where the screening would be done.

Tiny thought Guam had the most beautiful beaches in the world…brilliant white sand…beaches, Tiny would later discover, would make the beaches of Hawaii (including Waikiki) blanch in comparison. The crew's new orders called for a short stop at Pearl Harbor before going on to California. The 36 departed Guam December 16 and arrived at Pearl Harbor December 29. Crossing the International Date Line on an easterly course gave them the day back they had lost earlier. Since the crew crossed the date line December 25, they celebrated Christmas, 1945 twice, but hardly in the traditional manner. They ate the same menu, Spam rather than turkey and dressing, along with the customary ration of dehydrated potatoes.

World War II...Sea Duty

Once at Pearl Harbor, Tiny could hardly wait to don his whites and go ashore. That first liberty was not spent as one might think, guzzling beer and chasing girls. His first objective was the biggest steak he could find with mounds of mashed potatoes (made fresh; not powdered), topped off with a super large banana split! With that properly stowed, Tiny waddled back to the ship thinking of nothing else he cared to do on that trip ashore. He knew there would be plenty of opportunities to sightsee and do the town, which he did New Year's Eve.

The last leg of Tiny's dreamed about, talked about, written about, and until then only imagined journey began January 3, 1946. Nine days later, the sailors on 36 anchored in the harbor at San Pedro, California, where Tiny thought he had died and gone to Heaven! Like many of the other sailors, Tiny could not contain his tears of joy.

Though being home was exciting for Tiny, he had a lot for which to be thankful. In 16 months at sea there were many times when he and his fellow sailors were in critical situations when the outcome might have been different to have ended tragically. They participated in 10 invasions and many small skirmishes. Tiny had received no injury from hostile fire. His only injury came as the result of a souvenir hunt in the Philippines. Cutting a section of the rising sun from a downed Japanese Zero wing skin, Tiny cut his finger on a jagged edge. As the situation turned out, that was one souvenir Tiny carried with him the rest of his life...the scar!

Since he had received his training in the Eastern part of the country and had shipped out from Galveston, Texas, Tiny found seeing California for the first time January 12, 1945 memorable. The weather, as he soon learned, was typical of Southern California winters. Like General MacArthur, that day Tiny promised himself (as he had promised the Filipinos), he would return.

Tiny remained aboard the 36 until January 16, at which time he was transferred to the Naval base at nearby Terminal Island for further processing to the United States Naval Separation Center in Memphis, Tennessee.

Having spent 18 months on the 36 in close proximity with other men under trying times and frightful circumstances, leaving the ship Tiny learned the meaning of "parting is such sweet sorrow". Tears were in Tiny's eyes as he walked down that gangplank for what he knew would be his last time. In some ways Tiny found that parting as difficult, and perhaps more difficult than leaving home for the adventure in the 1st place. Tiny saluted "Old Glory" 1 last time at the mast where it seemed so long ago he had "run up" the flag on the 36 for the 1st time. He then turned and walked to the bus that waited to carry him to Terminal Island.

Decades later in his final years, Tiny still would feel a little burst of pride as he remembered that 1st flag raising ceremony. The flag was then and always remained special to Tiny. He thought contempt displayed for the US flag by other Americans was an insult to every American who ever served in time of war or peace. To Tiny, the flag stood for what is the greatest land in the world. Although Tiny, as well as anyone else at times, may not have been in total agreement with politicians and their policies, he always felt proud, as well as fortunate to be an American.

At Terminal Island many other men like Tiny waited to be processed. They fell out daily for muster. Due to a typographical error, Tiny came close to being absent at the first roll call. Someone had added a "y" to the end of his last name. As a result, the Master at Arms pronounced his last name "Gillum-ee". After he repeated the misspelled name for the 2nd or 3rd time, Tiny wised up, and realized he was being called. Tiny called the error to the attention of the Master at Arms telling him his last name was "Gillum". The misspelling was corrected.

At Terminal Island no regular duty assignments existed. At muster each day the Master at Arms would call for volunteers (housecleaning, policing up the area, etc.). Having learned his lesson about "volunteering", Tiny remained silent each time the call went out. Enough of the other men volunteered to fill duty roster. Tiny was never appointed.

A packet of 22 men of which Tiny was one were scheduled to be processed through the Memphis separation center. Designated draft #377, these 22 men were put under the supervision of a Chief Baker, who was the highest rated petty officer in the draft. He, in turn, appointed one of his own men, a Baker 3rd Class, to be his assistant. That turned out to be a problem for Tiny during their trip to Tennessee. The chief encountered personal problems prior to the departure and was granted an emergency leave. Since his assistant was already familiar with the proceedings, he was appointed to replace the chief, although, Tiny outranked him. The decision seemed appropriate at the time. Additionally, Tiny had no desire to make an issue out of the situation. The men were a jubilant bunch as they boarded the train. Everything was going just fine.

On the morning of January 23, the train stopped at Carrizozo, New Mexico to take on water. Tiny asked one of the crewmen how long they would be there. He was told "20 to 30 minutes, minimum."

Within sight of the train, but across a field, Tiny could see a grocery store. Such a short distance and with plenty of time, according to the train crewman, Tiny decided to run over and make a purchase (accompanied by a coxswain by the name of Robert Satterfield). They had just paid for some liquid refreshment consisting of a fifth of whiskey and a case of beer, when they heard the train whistle. Gathering their purchases, the two men rushed out to discover their train was about 2 blocks down the line and rapidly gaining speed!

In 1946 Carrizozo was just what one would think...a watering stop on the Katy line. No cabs! No buses! And few private cars! Tiny and his companion wore dungarees and neither had on a coat. A cold January morning in Carrizozo, the men's first order of business was to return their purchases in exchange for warmer clothing. The warmest clothing item they could find was sweaters. The store proprietor told Satterfield and Tiny other servicemen had missed their train there in similar fashion and had made their way to Clovis, New Mexico about 180 miles away where there was an air base. At the air base, the two sailors thought they would be channeled in the right direction.

Satterfield and Tiny hired a local rancher with a pickup truck to take them to Clovis. Unlike pickups of today, his truck was built for two, not three people. Tiny and his new found friend alternated between the seat and the bed of the truck in 2-hour shifts. While in the bed of the truck, each one would huddle in a corner with no more than a blanket to ward off the cold winds.

Reaching Clovis Monday morning, January 24, the two men went immediately to report to the military police. After listening to their sad tale of woe, they took Satterfield and Tiny to the air base. That's when their problems really began! The Provost Marshal would not accept their word and insisted they be treated as absent without official leave (AWOL). With each of their personal items confiscated, except for a comb and handkerchief, Satterfield and Tiny were tossed in the guardhouse!

The Provost Marshal's main problem with the story of the two sailors was the fact that he could not accept a lower rated man being in charge of our draft. Even with the specific details they provided, their words were meaningless to the provost. He could not reconcile Tiny's being part of a packet commanded by a lower ranked noncommissioned officer! Unable to explain that to the provost's satisfaction made the two sailors "suspect" in his mind.

In the guardhouse, Satterfield and Tiny had the company of six airmen. The airmen charged with a variety of military infractions and were waiting for courts martial. Soon Satterfield and Tiny learned the airmen had been waiting up to 6 months, which offered them no reason for celebration. They had no crime charges, only the suspicion of being AWOL. No charges could be filed unless, or until they had a reasonable basis for doing so. The Provost Marshal, an Air Force captain, could not swear charges with no more than his suspicious nature. But, that did nothing to achieve Satterfield's and Tiny's freedom. The Provost Marshal told the two sailors he would contact Naval authorities to confirm or deny their story.

Meanwhile, they remained "guests" of the United States Air Force, albeit unwillingly.

While in the custody of the Air Force, Satterfield and Tiny found daily routines dull to boring. Allowed to leave their "confines" only 3 times a day, they were marched under guard to the mess hall and back. This was quite a comedown from the excitement of the high seas and a "real war" that, in their opinion, they had fought while their captors luxuriated in the comforts of stateside service.

Being Navy with no charges filed against them, Satterfield and Tiny were exempt from daily details. They spent their days indoors patiently waiting for the airmen to complete their daily duties so they could play Pinochle. At least during this time, Tiny learned to play double deck, which he found more challenging than the single deck variety. That, too, was small compensation for so much loss of time on a trip that should have been a happy event. When "lights out" came, Tiny spend long hours contemplating. *What the hell,* Tiny asked himself. *Why is a sailor in an Air Force guardhouse, when he should be in Memphis picking up an honorable discharge?* Like anyone in service, Tiny experienced times when he thought the duty unfair, unpleasant, or unnecessary but not once had he landed in the brig…on report, yes…punished with extra duty, yes…but a "military criminal"—that was not Tiny!!! He also kept remembering Mam-Maw's admonition about flies, sugar, and honey.

After about the 3rd day Tiny began to think he would be there forever. *Why,* he wondered, *could the Provost Marshal not simply pick up a telephone and confirm or discount our explanation?* For decades Tiny continued to feel a sense of anger about the situation.

After 3 days, the train had arrived in Memphis and a report would have been made to officials at the separation center. At last, Tiny decided to try talking to the captain to make a last desperate appeal. To Tiny's surprise, he granted the sailor an audience! Tiny learned quickly, the captain had done NOTHING! He might as well have been in a Mexican jail cell. The captain had no consideration for Tiny's rights, civil or military. At that point Tiny wished he had given more attention to the Uniform Code of Military Justice, the so called "G.I. Bill of Rights", but common sense dictated Tiny must have had SOME rights.

Ultimately, Tiny could no longer contain his anger. Captain, or not, Tiny let him know how he felt about him, his stinking guardhouse, and his lack of decency. Tiny thought his confrontation would seal his fate but at that moment, Tiny didn't care. Although the captain expressed no feelings of decency or remorse, for some reason Tiny could not explain, the captain agreed to pursue the matter. Two days later, January 29, Satterfield and Tiny were informed that a Navy shore patrol would arrive January 31 to take the sailors into custody.

After an anxious weekend, on Monday the shore patrol arrived. This made Tiny one happy individual! In all fairness to the captain, he did mumble an apology to the sailors as they were being taken away by the shore patrol. As Satterfield and Tiny passed through the main gate, they breathed a sigh of relief.

Taken to Santa Fe's Navy Recruiting Station in the city hall (which, coincidently, also housed the jail), the two sailors were assigned a cell. The officer in charge of the recruiting station, though not present, had left instructions for the boatswain on duty to put them up there because they had no authorization to rent a room in one of the local hotels, or to allow the sailors to do so. Thinking, *well, here we go again*; the two sailors spent a long and sleepless night as "guests" of the city of Santa Fe—sleepless for reasons other than pure frustration. During the night, the cell next to the sailors was filled with drunks, vagrants, and who knows what else! With all the yelling and fighting going on, no one could have slept. At about 1000 hours, Tuesday morning, Satterfield and Tiny were escorted to the lieutenant in charge of the recruiting station. Once more, they recited all the details they had recited so many times before. They provided answers to specific answers about the draft they had been traveling with, its point of origination, destination, where and why they missed the train, and the entire guardhouse episode.

Although the lieutenant had reservations about the matter, he showed compassion, unlike Provost Marshal. He cut new orders for Satterfield and Tiny, allowing them to continue to Memphis at their own expense with authorization for them to travel in dungarees. Remember, this was their only attire. The new orders would possibly keep the two sailors from being charged with being out of uniform along the way, and subsequent arrest!

Noting that their new orders instructed them to "Depart Santa Fe on February 2", Satterfield and Tiny called the lieutenant's attention to the fact that they would have to stay over one more night. They further expressed their desire to be on the way and out of the lieutenant's way pronto. Whether for his own concern, or the concern of the sailors, the lieutenant granted permission. The two men had a one-way ticket to Memphis and left on the next bus, which happened to be the last one that day.

On the bus, Satterfield and Tiny began to see a little light at the end of a long, dark tunnel. At each rest stop along the way, they stepped off the bus expecting, in fact, hoping to be challenged. Since they had authorization to be in dungarees, Tiny thought being challenged would have done the two more good than harm, if only so they could smile at their confusion. To Satterfield and Tiny's consternation, none of the armband wearing soldiers or sailors paid us a second glance. The bus pulled into Memphis February 3. The two sailors hastened to the separation center, wondering how the next chapter of this travesty would unfold.

At the separation center, no one seemed concerned about what happened. They displayed no interest in the men's plight or the consequences. The attitude of the staff was "We're here to process you. You're here to be processed, so what's all this talk about missing a train and being put in a guardhouse?" They seemed to be saying, "Shut up, and get moving sailor." That was almost as good as hearing "Welcome home, Sailor!"

Asking if their gear had been turned in, the two sailors were instructed to check with the Master at Arms of the barracks to which they had been assigned. A burly old chief at the barracks pointed to a room off to one side, saying, "If it was turned in, it would be in there."

A brief search turned up the gear, intact. Grabbing a couple of empty bunks to wait out the events, Satterfield and Tiny felt such relief that they broke out in uncontrolled laughter!

With time on his hands, Tiny decided what a good time to explore what charges he might lodge, if any, against the Provost Marshal at the Clovis Air Force Base. Referred to a legal officer, a bright young man who was seemingly well versed in military justice, Tiny listed the events and answered detailed questions about what did and did not occur at Clovis. After reviewing his notes, the legal office offered the opinion that Tiny had "a very good case", and that he would be glad to prosecute the claim. However, there was one hitch. To prosecute, Tiny would have to defer discharge and stay in the Navy until the case was settled. This could take 6 months or more! Because, at the time, Tiny valued his freedom a lot more than revenge, he chose to drop the case. On the processing Tiny was approached with an offer to sign up for 4 more years. He was promised Quartermaster 1st Class immediately and chief within 18 months. As eager has Tiny had been to get into the Navy, that desire was nothing compared to his present desire to get out of the Navy. Tiny thought he would have declined if they had offered to make him admiral on the spot.

On Wednesday, February 6, 1946, after 2 years, 4 months, and 28 days, Tiny had an honorable discharge in his hand. His small contribution during World War II imbued Tiny with memories he could not have otherwise had...memories he treasured...and experiences he could never forget. Tiny was proud to have served his country in whatever limited manner he served.

At Salzburg, Austria, on July 4, 1945, Tiny was told that Infantry General Michael O'Daniel, addressed his troops. Among O'Daniel's comments were the words, "Any man who has faced an armed enemy in the defense of his country, is a hero in my eyes."

If that be true, Tiny's boyhood fantasy of being a hero came true. He was certain that the general would agree that all the sailors aboard the 36 faced an armed enemy in defense of their country.

Tiny left the Navy with no regrets. Given the same time, the same circumstances, and the same options, he felt he would serve his country again. For Tiny, though he experienced moments of concern, moments of fear, and moments of despair; he also experienced just as many moments of elation, gaiety, camaraderie, and joviality…and these positive experiences were the easiest to remember. Serving with the officers and crew of LSM 36 and the Group 5 staff was a pleasure for Tiny. Hoping he had been of some benefit to his country, Tiny hastened back to Ashland to commence another chapter in the life of a common man.

***

CHAPTER 5

The Attitude Adjustment Years

For Tiny, the train ride from Memphis to Ashland was filled with the anxiety of going home to friends and relatives, but with reservations. Three and one half years had passed since he had quit his job in Baltimore, of which less than a month had been spent at home. Decades later Tiny believed growing up in any community is about the same for everyone. Until that eventful day when a person ventures forth on his or her own that community, whether a country village, or a giant Metropolis, represents the center of the universe.

People leave hometowns bearing the memories of childhood, and return expecting everything to be unchanged…to discover the streets they once thought so big have become smaller…the buildings they once thought so magnificent have lost their sheen…and the people, once so young, have aged. The river that, in childhood, was the mainstream of life has turned muddy and sluggish. Realizing that everything does change takes individuals a few days at best, or a few years at worst. At some point in that transition a person realizes that he or she cannot revert to what he or she was before and that like the streets, the buildings, and the river, that individual too has changed.

When Tiny came to the realization that circumstances would never be the same again, he became confused. Making the adjustment from civilian life to wartime military life was difficult for Tiny, but nothing compared to reversing the procedure. Uncertain as Tiny was about what to do, where to do what, and thinking there was no rush to do anything, Tiny decided to kick back, relax, and enjoy his freedom.

The local voters had voted Boyd County "dry" in Tiny's absence. Unable to buy as much as a beer in Ashland, Tiny crossed the river to Ironton, Ohio for his liquor. *What a bum rap*, he thought. *A guy home from the service has to leave the state just to get drunk!*

During the next few months Tiny tried, and tried hard, to drink Ohio dry. Cliff had preceded Tiny home, having been discharged from the Army. Thus, Tiny had a convenient, complacent, and cooperative drinking partner. Cliff and Tiny joined the 52-20 club, so called because Congress authorized returning veterans to receive $20 a week for up to 52 weeks as a subsistence allowance during their period of readjustment. Twenty dollars today seems insignificant, but in 1946 that amount would buy a lot of beer.

With the help of Frank Pennington (Tiny's new stepfather), Tiny bought an old Chrysler automobile that someone had converted to a pickup. Not much to look at, the car carried Cliff and Tiny to and from their drinking assignments. A two-toned beauty, Tiny named his car "Ookie" (for what reason, he didn't know). The cab of the vehicle was blue with the bed pink. Being his first motor vehicle, Ookie cost Tiny

$200, a sum that pales by comparison to what the cost would have been had Cliff and Tiny had to travel back and forth to Ironton by bus.

Ookie soon became a familiar sight in Ironton, and was known by all from "Ginn's Gin Mill" on the west to "Ritzy Raye's" on the east side of town. The Marshal of Coal Grove, Ohio, Jack Dalton, did not share Tiny's appreciation for Ookie any more than he did Tiny's drinking habits.

Marshal Dalton usually could be found aboard his motorcycle somewhere between Coal Grove and Ironton behind a billboard. On the return leg of a journey to Ironton, he pulled Tiny over for a broken taillight. He didn't give Tiny a citation, but he did say, "Get this blue goose across the river, and don't come back unless or until that taillight is fixed!" Repairing a taillight was not, in Tiny's mind, something he had to do NOW. Fixing the taillight could wait until he finished his assigned duty to drink the town dry.

Next night, true to his self-imposed obligation, Tiny was off to Ironton, broken taillight and all. About a quarter of a mile from the Ironton city limits, Marshal Dalton once again pulled Tiny over. Leaving Ookie's engine running, Tiny waited while the officer shut down his motorcycle, put down the kick stand, and sauntered toward Tiny's truck. Watching in the mirror, Tiny waited until the officer was about even with the rear of his truck, then gunned the engine, and sped across the line into Ironton. *He can wait,* Tiny thought to himself, *for another time to get his revenge on me.* With no jurisdiction in Ironton, Tiny had outsmarted the officer.

Later, knowing the officer would be waiting for him, Tiny drove out of Ironton to the south and across the river at Russell, Kentucky. Somewhere or sometime between discovering they could make beer a little faster than he could drink it and before his membership in the 52-20 club expired, Tiny decided the time had come to get a job.

    The local market was not very good, but American Rolling Mill Company (ARMCO) had a policy favoring veterans. Cliff and Tiny both submitted applications. In time, both of them were offered jobs as stand-by laborers at $1.05 per hour (a decent rate for that period of time in that place). Stand-by laborers worked wherever needed...foundry...hearth furnace ...or elsewhere to replace unskilled laborers, who were on vacation or out because of illness. As the work varied, so did the hours. Everything depended on vacancies occurring. At the end of each work day, the men were required to check with the job assigner to learn if and where they might be working the next day. This system was supposed to put men in line for permanent jobs when such vacancies occurred. Tiny knew one man who had been doing that work for several years and that man's chances for permanent work was slim and none. When Cliff and Tiny decided to decline the offer, the man at Armco's desk seemed very surprised, saying "Many men in Ashland would give their right arm to work for Armco." The man may have been right, but Cliff and Tiny walked away.

    After exhausting every possibility in the Ashland area, Cliff and Tiny hopped a bus to Dayton, Ohio where chances looked better. Ookie was left behind in the junk yard, having fallen victim to old age and hard work. They got off the bus in Dayton without the price of a room for the night, but with one ace in the hole.

    The son and daughter of one of their mother's friends were living and working in Dayton. They kindly put up Cliff and Tiny for a few nights while they canvassed the area for work. Not long before their welcome was sure to run out, Cliff and Tiny bumped into a cousin named Burl, son of Uncle Lonnie, their father's brother. He and his friend, Tommie, had a sleeping room. They invited Cliff and Tiny to join them. Neither of them had worked long enough to get a paycheck, but they were employed by Frigidaire, a division of General Motors. Thus, the four men pooled their meager resources, stocking up on peanut butter, bread, and cheese. Sandwiches of this limited larder were beginning to be very hard to swallow by the time Burl and Tommie received their first paycheck. White Tower was the McDonald's of that era. The four men headed there first after receiving the first paydays.

A few days later Cliff and Tiny were hired by Delco Manufacturing Company, also a division of General Motors and the manufacturer of automobile parts. Cliff went to the grinding department while Tiny drew the shock absorber assembly line. As a part of the assembly line, Tiny operated a pneumatic screwdriver from 8 a.m. to 4 p.m., with a 12-minute lunch, for which he was paid his normal hourly rate. His job was to attach a metal nameplate to each shock absorber, as it traveled down the assembly line.

Smoking was permitted on the job but breaks were not and no smoking was allowed in the restrooms. Both hands being occupied by his job, Tiny had little time to smoke. Each time he made an effort to get ahead enough to light up; the conveyor seemed to simply run faster. Tiny found no way to get ahead of the line. Then one day Tiny realized there was another machine exactly like his but the other machine had not been in operation at any time since Tiny started. Dumb, yes. Stupid, no! Realizing he was doing two men's work for one man's pay, Tiny stepped back, and lit up. Seconds later, as the units began to show up down the line without nameplates, the lead man came down on Tiny with both feet. Tiny made his point about two men's work and one man's pay. When the supervisor got control of his blood pressure, he started up the other machine, and the two men finished the day with both machines in operation.

The next day though, Tiny ended up doing a different job in a different area. Tiny's fate was sealed by his behavior the day before. From that day forward, his supervisor handed him nothing but dead end tasks, from which there could be no advancement. Finally, Tiny quit blaming his superiors for refusing to allow him to show what he could do.

National Cash Register (NCR) was considered the most desirable company to work for in the Dayton area, so Tiny went there. A kind gentleman at the employment desk gave him an application to complete. After laboring through the questions, Tiny returned the application. He said, "Thanks, have a seat and enjoy something to read until we call you."

The back wall was lined with books, enough to shame most small public libraries. About an hour later Tiny turned to another man, who had been reading when he came in, and asked, "How long do they expect us to read before we are called?"

He said, "I don't know. This is my 3rd day of reading." That was all Tiny needed to hear. He quietly closed his book and walked out.

Later Tiny ran into a friend from Ashland, Buck Sparks. Buck had arrived in town after Tiny left Delco. He too rented a room at the same place where Tiny and his roommates reside. Buck and Tiny ended up answering the same help wanted ad for a job at Inland Manufacturing. Learning that this company too was a part of General Motors, Tiny figured he had no chance because of his experience at Delco and that he would surely be blacklisted. To his surprise, Buck and Tiny both were hired.

The two friends became inseparable companions, sharing many experiences in the bars around town, especially the west end of town. The west end was where the "Friendly Inn" was located. That's where they hung out. Tiny always remembered the words on the front door entrance, "Meet your friends at the friendly inn...where the elite meet to eat." Not too many of the "elite" ate there, but Buck and Tiny did meet some very fine people at the inn. On one occasion, they prevented a guy from being rolled by a couple of thugs and later helped break up a fight. This earned respect from the management and made them look more like heroes than the "good time Charlies" they had been called in other places.

Things went well at Inland until one day when Tiny was assigned dip tank duty. Having had that assignment before, Tiny disliked and feared the job. An acid solution was used in the tank to aid in the cleaning of steering wheels. Although gloves were worn, preventing contact with the solution during the dipping process was almost impossible. Tiny did not want any part of the rash and constant itch that often resulted from that job.

Tiny decided to express his feelings about the new job assignment to the foreman (diplomatically, of course), recalling the incident at Delco. When Tiny explained his concerns, the foreman responded, "I don't know why they hire hillbilly sons of bitches like you anyway!"

Immediately Tiny hit the foreman in the mouth! Recovering, the foreman grabbed a steering wheel from the line intending to charge Tiny. Buck wrested the wheel from the foreman's hand just as Tiny hit him again.

After the foreman had been taken to the first aid station and after the dust had settled, Tiny went back to work expecting a call to the personnel office where he would be given his separation pay. In due time the call came. There, instead of being confronted by a foul-mouthed slob, Tiny was asked to "tell his side of the story" (Tiny assumed he had already heard the other side.). Thinking being treated with courtesy and what appeared to be concern was strange, Tiny related what happened. After listening attentively, the gentleman told Tiny to return to the job he had been doing before the incident, which he did though still puzzled.

In a few days the truth leaked out. The foul-mouthed foreman had been transferred to the day shift and to a different area on probation. Apparently he had been the cause of similar incidents, but no one had challenged him until then.

After about 3 months at Inland, Tiny was still in that mindless state, unsure of what he wanted to do and where he wanted to do what. Tiny was still dreaming of going back to California, though the desire was not expressed aloud. Buck, too, was in a bit of a dither. The cute little redhead he had met at the Friendly Inn was pressuring him to marry her, so he too was ready to leave the area. The two friends began talking about a trip to Las Vegas in search of rich and beautiful divorcees. However, what they really did was quit their jobs and migrate back to Ashland. Tiny's Brother Cliff had more sense staying with Delco.

Back in Ashland, Tiny applied for reinstatement of his 52-20 checks, which had been put on hold while he was working. Reinstatement was not easy. To qualify, one had to come up with some likely sounding story of why he was out of work again and also had to make a visible attempt to seek employment. Regulations required the former military man to contact at least three potential employers each week. This made some learn to lie, if they did not know how to do so before. In a town the size of Ashland, three lies per week can compound awfully fast, and suddenly one discovers that all resources have been exhausted.

When Tiny exhausted his resources he knew he had to seek work...nah, he had to FIND work...and soon! He ended up driving a cab with no salary, just straight commission. The cabs had governors set for 40 miles per hour, which made for undesirable conditions when one was trying to hustle for business. The governor ended up being Tiny's nemesis.

On one occasion Tiny was flagged down by two preachers who were trying to get to a funeral in Huntington. They offered Tiny a bonus of $20 if he could get them there in 45 minutes or less. One of the other cab drivers had told Tiny how to break the governor, using nothing more than the accelerator. Thus, he accepted the bonus offer and assured the preachers there would be no problem getting them there in time. Just as Tiny had been told, slacking off the gas (just as the speedometer needle hit 40) and then "slamming" the gas to the floor broke the governor. That trick earned Tiny the bonus. Unfortunately, the cab company's mechanic also knew the trick. Tiny ended up on the street again looking for work.

In November of 1946, Cliff married Norma Jean Ryan from Spring Valley, Ohio. On their honeymoon Cliff brought his new bride home to

Ashland for the first time. Cliff had a friend, Bill Dillon, whose company he truly enjoyed. During Cliff and Norma's visit, naturally, the newlyweds, Bill, and Tiny made an excursion to some of their old hangouts in Ironton. At the time, of course, Tiny thought bringing your drinking buddy along on a night out during one's honeymoon was normal. Bill, after a few drinks, as he was known to have done before, got rowdy. The bartender at Ginn's Gin Mill called the police. When the police showed up Bill gave them a bad time, Cliff butted in, and they both ended up in jail. Norma and Tiny spent all night getting them out. What an impression that must have made on the pretty, unsuspecting new bride brought home to Ashland for the first time!

In time Tiny got another job for Tristate Painting Company under a government program providing "on the job training". Part of the G.I. Bill of Rights, trainees were paid $20 a week maximum. The government kicked in an extra $20 for a stipulated period of time. Tiny never found out how long the training would last. However, he was told the government checks took 2 to 3 weeks to commence. When his government checks hadn't arrived after 5 or 6 weeks, Tiny went to the company to inquire about the delay. He discovered company employees had not bothered to finish processing his application. Thus, he had been working his buns off for $20 a week. The work was hot and tiring. At that point Tiny gave up any hope of becoming a journeyman painter.

His next employment went down the tube when the union and company reached an impasse. In those days, if the union called a strike, a man walked out even if not a member of the union. To do otherwise, crossing picket lines could get one killed.

When Tiny realized the strike would not end before his resources ran out and without income, he started seeking employment again. During this time, Tiny's cousin Jahanny called his attention to an ad he had seen. The ad read, "Work your way to California and return!" Working his way to California appealed to Tiny! Returning did not! Jahanny and Tiny applied, and were both hired. This job was straight commission and turned out to be a sleazy deal. Young people, like Tiny and Jahanny, were taught to lay a sad tale of woe on people to entice them to buy a magazine subscription. Tiny hated the work. After 2 weeks, he had sold few subscriptions and he and his cousin were no more than 75 or 80 miles from home. At that rate, Tiny knew California would have broken off and fallen into the ocean before they arrived. The year 1947 was drawing to a close. Tiny was no closer to California than he had been a year or more before.

With a few more weeks of his 52-20 checks remaining, Tiny filed for reinstatement. While in this state of affairs, he met the girl who would become his wife, Alieta May Phillips. She was only 17 years old, 5 years Tiny's junior. Her parents did not agree with their marriage plans. They wanted a better candidate for a son-in-law; and later in retrospect, Tiny guessed they did have a point.

The state of Kentucky as well as West Virginia required parental consent, if the bride to be was less than 18 years of age. The couple had no other option but to elope. Their plans were for Alieta to take the bus to Ashland from her home in Huntington. Together, they would bus elsewhere, lie about her age, and tie the knot.

As Tiny waited anxiously for Alieta's arrival, little did he know that their plans had been discovered. Oh, yes, she showed up...and right on time…but not on a bus. She was in the family car, along with her parents! They told Tiny they were taking Alieta May to visit her grandparents and an aunt in Phoenix, Arizona. They said they planned on remaining there until the end of March when Alieta May would turn 18. Then they would return and the marriage plans could go forward. Tiny could do little but resign himself to a waiting game (or so her parents thought).

Alieta May gave Tiny the phone number of her aunt, which allowed them to keep in touch in the interim. Tiny made no further effort to find employment because, by then he was determined to go back to California in April. Deep down he knew the plans of Alieta May's family to return would not come to pass. He knew if Alieta May and he were to be married, the location of the marriage would be somewhere other than Kentucky or West Virginia. With very little money (surely not enough for bus or train fare), Tiny decided to hitchhike. Perhaps, because misery loves company, Tiny discussed his plans with all his friends, inviting anyone interested to join him.

Foolishly, Tiny thought several of his friends would "sign up" to join him on his trip hitchhiking west. On the fateful morning of his departure, April 27, Tiny was genuinely disappointed to find no one was waiting for him on the corner of 29th and Winchester Avenue, the prearranged starting point. Then he heard a voice call his name. The voice he heard was that of Bill Brumfield, suitcase in hand! *Well*, Tiny thought, *at least someone else wants to try greener pastures*. Although Bill and Tiny had gone to school together, they had never been very close friends. Tiny was surprised by Bill's presence, as he had a wife and small child. Bill assured Tiny he would telephone his wife later in the day and that he would send for her and the baby as soon as he got settled in California.

Bill and Tiny discussed and agreed on some ground rules for the trip: there would be no drinking; clothes would be maintained, so they wouldn't look like bums; and, they would be clean shaven at all times. They also agreed on what their story would be, in the event they were challenged by the police anywhere along the way. Tiny's earlier confrontation with the military police at Carrizozo had suitably convinced him of the need for preparation. Those things settled the two men were on their way.

Bill and Tiny's first lift took them to Saint Louis, Missouri. At Saint Louis they rented a motel for the night. Next morning, suitably dressed, shaved, and bathed, they "hung out their thumbs" in anticipation of that day's events. Meals, for the most part, consisted of baloney sandwiches, because they had agreed to subsist on such a diet, giving preference to maintaining their appearances. To anyone who asked, the men were on their way to Phoenix, where they had jobs lined up.

After a couple of hours on the highway, Bill and Tiny caught a ride to some insignificant point. Hours later, they got another ride. At long last a trucker picked up the two travelers, saying he would be on Route 66 to Oklahoma City, Oklahoma, but had to drop south to Route 80 for a scheduled stop in Midland, Texas. He added that, after a few hours in Midland, he would then drive straight through to El Paso. Thinking that would save them a night's lodging, they opted to ride along with the trucker. Moving in any direction was better than standing at the side of the road, while being ridiculed and having people aim their cars at you…just to see you run!

The Attitude Adjustment Years

The trucker, along with his passengers, rolled into Midland about 2:00 a.m. He told Bill and Tiny that unloading would take about 2 hours and that after unloading, if Bill and Tiny were interested, they could rejoin him for the trip to El Paso. *Good idea*, they thought. They were dropped off to look for a place to spend the next few hours, out of sight and out of the way, they hoped. Locating an all-night service station, Bill and Tiny obtained the operator's permission to "sit it out". Settled down in the corner out of the way, both travelers soon fell asleep.

An hour or so later, Bill and Tiny were roused from sleep by a flashlight and the voice of one of Midland's "finest". Explaining that they had permission to be there, and backed up by the operator's agreement served no purpose. There must have been too much moonlight that night and this bullheaded bastard was too cowardly to rustle cattle. Instead, he rustled Bill and Tiny. Taken to the police station, they were stripped of their belongings and shoved into a cell with a few other unfortunates...Carrizozo revisited, Tiny thought! Nothing they could say had any effect. They had to wait for the arrival of the "chief" of Midland's "finest". He would decide their fate.

About 8:30 a.m. the jailer took only Bill to the chief's office for questioning. A few minutes later, Tiny had his turn in the barrel. The chief's words to Tiny were "We're charging you guys with vagrancy."

"If you do, you won't do it legally," Tiny replied.

Tiny then pointed out they were clean and reasonably dressed, did not look like vagrants, and that, moreover, Bill and he were carrying more than $40 when arrested. Tiny didn't know at the time but Texas law then allowed a man to carry a weapon if "beyond his county of residence, he was carrying a significant sum of money, with significant defined as $20, or more. Whether the chief knew that, Tiny wasn't sure.

When Tiny "smarted off" to the chief, the chief lost his temper, and about the only thing he had, in sufficient volume to lose, were T and S (temper and stupidity). "You're a smart ass, ain't you!" he shouted.

With concern for his personal safety, Tiny lowered his voice and explained how he and Bill were on their way to Phoenix, where they had jobs lined up, and offered the phone number of Alieta's aunt, by which the chief could confirm the fact. The remainder of the chief's and Tiny's verbal exchange serves no purpose to this narrative. However, the conversation ended with Bill and Tiny being "escorted" out of town. Offered a ride to the city limits, they elected to walk. *At least*, they thought, *we'll walk out with our dignity intact*. They headed for the highway with a Midland police car following. At the city limits, the two travelers waved a cordial goodbye, as they thought, *Boy, we would love to shove it in your face*.

Midland! According to Tiny, the town's name should have been "shitland!" Anyone who has driven through that God forsaken den of rattlesnakes, scorpions, locoweed, and sagebrush, populated by people of like nature, can attest to the residents' total lack of saving graces. Later, after his introduction to the town "hospitalities", Tiny was told that Midland is a land rich in oil, plus enormous cattle ranches. *Too bad they don't spend a few dollars civilizing their public servants,* Tiny thought.

Once outside Midland, Bill and Tiny caught a ride to a small place called Hilltop, where they indulged themselves with food and beverages, While at Hilltop Tiny overheard a man say he was on his way to El Paso. When asked whether he would give the two a lift, the man said, "yes." Seated in the man's car, they were immediately challenged by what Tiny first thought to be a drunkard demanding identification. Rather than create a scene, Tiny produced his I.D. To Tiny's surprise, the man turned out to be a Texas Ranger (hardly the image most people would have of such "stalwarts"). The ranger offered to take the travelers off the hands of their latest benefactor if they were bothering him. Fortunately, the benefactor said, "no."

Bill and Tiny were soon on their way to El Paso without further hindrance or incidence. Once in El Paso they decided to invest a portion of their remaining resources on a bus ticket to Phoenix. They reached Phoenix Thursday, April 29 to a cordial welcome from Alieta, plus her aunt and uncle...but hardly warm or cordial from her parents...who, to Tiny's surprise, did not seem too happy to see him!

While in Phoenix, Alieta's aunt and uncle housed and fed Bill and Tiny but without any such cooperation from her parents. Tiny could not understand why! Alieta's parent's told Tiny if he and Alieta married, the union would be without their consent. Alieta's aunt disagreed. She offered to help with wedding plans and said her home would be made available for the purpose. For once, common sense prevailed! Tiny decided to go on to California, get a job and get settled; after which, he would return to Phoenix for the wedding.

Alieta's father, still adamant, said, "We do not agree with any of this. The only thing you will get from us is $100."

Once more, Tiny's fuse was lit! He guessed Alieta's father thought Tiny wanted to marry his daughter for "his" money. By the time her father drew his next breath, he knew otherwise!

Early morning May 1, 1948, Bill and Tiny hit the road again. Soon they caught a ride that took them to Lomita, near Long Beach, California. There they rented a room at the YMCA for 50 cents a night. Just as General MacArthur, "Tiny had returned!" Through all this, he gradually calmed down and, he thought, underwent a significant change in "attitude".

The attitude adjustment years were over. Tiny was ready to begin anew in a new environment.

***

CHAPTER 6

California...
The 1st Dozen Years

The Long Beach YMCA, though far removed (in distance and sophistication) from New York's Waldorf Astoria, was "home" for the moment until they could make other, more suitable, living accommodations.

Tiny's only contact to California was a name: Bob Loughland. Bob, a staff quartermaster assigned to 36 had once told Tiny that he lived in Compton, California, adding "if you are ever near there, look me up."

Learning that Compton was only about 10 miles from Long Beach, Tiny dialed information for Bob's number. He was able to contact him Saturday evening. Bob seemed pleased by the call, and invited Bill and Tiny to visit Sunday, the next day.

Latecomers to Southern California may never have seen the Big Red Cars. The system was abandoned in the '60's. Most of the tracks were pulled up and sold for scrap metal, by what warped sense of logic, Tiny didn't know. The system was a magnificent, all electric (nonpolluting) interurban railroad that simply gave way to freeways. At the time of Tiny's arrival to California, the railroad system served all the communities of Southern California from Long Beach to Riverside, plus Ventura, Santa Monica, and many Orange County communities.

Early Sunday afternoon Bill and Tiny boarded one of those Big Red Cars. In moments they were in the company of Bob, his wife Pat, and their daughters, Debbie and Kerrie. The families made their guests feel genuinely welcome and, little did they know, they probably saved the two men from eminent starvation when they invited them to join them for a backyard barbecue. That was Bill and Tiny's first home cooked meal in several days and first real meal in California. After dinner, Bob asked about the men's finances. Tiny admitted they were down to their last 27 cents. Without hesitation, Bob reached into his pocket and hauled out $20, asking if that would help tide them over. Moreover, he invited Bill and Tiny to move out of the YMCA and stay with his family a few days while searching for work. Without Bob's generosity, this tale might have had an altogether different ending!

Luckily, for Bill and Tiny, their employment search was not of a long duration. Using the Big Red Car, they concentrated on the immediate Los Angeles area, because they realized their chances would be much better there due to a more centralized industrial area.

Bill and Tiny returned to Compton and using part of the $20 Bob had so generously loaned them, they rented a sleeping room at $5 per week. Since the company did not hold back a week's pay, they knew they would be able to repay Bob on Friday and still have enough left over (from their joint earnings) to upgrade their Velveeta cheese/bologna diet!

The Davidson Company, headquartered in San Francisco, manufactured portable evaporative coolers (better known as "swamp coolers"), which at that time was the only product available for motorists travelling across the southwestern deserts. Because the market for these coolers was predominantly summer oriented, the company rented facilities there to meet peak demands, and then closed down as the market "cooled".

Tiny's job was "utility man". In other words, he worked where and as needed, which exposed him to various phases of all the manufacturing/testing operations. After about a week, Tiny's supervisors assigned him to tank installation a bit more critical than some of his previous tasks. Care had to be exercised in this step to prevent damage. Dents, although they did not affect operation of the device, were not tolerated. Production rates depended, apparently on the speed and efficiency with which this task could be performed. After no more than a day or two, Tiny fashioned a cylindrical tool that greatly simplified the job, while eliminating any risk of damage. His shift foreman rewarded him with a five cent hourly raise when he saw the line speed up. Although this only increased Tiny's weekly pay by $2, every little bit helps, as the old saying goes!

Soon a letter from Tiny's mother arrived asking whether Bill Brumfield was with him. Quite obviously Bill had not informed his wife, as he had promised, of either his whereabouts or his plans! Tiny showed Bill the letter, and told him he would not lie to his mother. That prompted Bill to call home (as he should have done long before). In a few days, he was on a bus headed for Ashland.

In mid-July, the company eliminated the night shift, which was an indication the time was fast approaching for the closing of the entire operation. Tiny's plans had been to be earning as much as possible by the time the closing occurred. This, he thought, would allow him to command a better wage on the next job he would be seeking. Deciding he had nothing to lose, Tiny confronted the foreman, demanding a 10 cent per hour raise. In reply, he reminded Tiny that the position was only a summer job and that the plant would be closing very soon. Tiny's response to the foreman was, "I know, but unless I get the raise, I will be gone Friday."

The plant manager approved the increase. The last two people to leave the plant upon closing were the foreman and Tiny. Although fully prepared for being out of work, the timing gave Tiny some anxious moments. The plant shut down Wednesday, August 4...and Alieta and Tiny were planning to be married Saturday, August 7! On Tiny's last day, the plant manager complimented him on the fine job he had done, and invited him to stay with the company. The new job would be in San Francisco with full relocation expenses included, but Tiny declined the offer, being perfectly happy with the climate in Southern California.

Upon Tiny's departure, he was given a very nice letter of recommendation and, as a parting gesture, the plant manager phoned a friend at Weber Showcase in Los Angeles, recommending Tiny for employment. In his later job search, Tiny visited Weber, but made no application because he lacked the patience to wait out the long, long line of applicants. Instead, hearing that North American Aviation in Downey had a few openings for sheet metal workers, Tiny hopped a bus, and headed for their employment office hoping for work in line with previous experience.

The lines at North American Aviation were just as long but, for some reason, they did not discourage Tiny as those at Weber Showcase had done. After a lengthy wait, they offered Tiny a job at $1.05 per hour. He accepted so quickly, the interviewer remarked, "You really do need a job, don't you?"

When Tiny told the interviewer he was being married on the following Saturday, he said, "Well then, we'll make that $1.10 per hour!"

Assigned to the Navy AJ-1 project, Tiny was told to report to work Tuesday, August 10. *This is my lucky day*, Tiny thought. Tiny's "luck" continued that day as he also met a guy named Thomas Arthur Marine Spence (known as Buster), from Oklahoma. Buster had a crop of bright red hair, and was about as likeable, laid back and happy go lucky as any man could be. He also owned an automobile! Even more important, he lived in Compton. In a day Tiny had landed a job, met a man who would become one of the best friends he would ever have, and solved his transportation problem getting to and from his new job!

Returning to his room at what, Tiny thought, was the end of a very eventful day, he had another surprise in store! A letter from Alieta informed Tiny that her parents had relented, and would be bringing her to Compton on Friday that same week. They arrived as scheduled, and Tiny and

Alieta were married the next day in a simple ceremony at one of the local Methodist churches. After the wedding, her parents treated the wedding party to dinner at Carl's by the Sea in Santa Monica. No mention was made of the "$100". Due to Tiny's having to report for work Tuesday, the honeymoon was short. The newlyweds spent that weekend in a motel on Long Beach Boulevard. On Monday, they rented a sleeping room in Compton where Buster was living.

A man is, Tiny thought decades later, *fortunate to have a few really "true" friends in his lifetime. Perhaps that is why we have only six pallbearers when that time comes...not many are fortunate to have more than six friends.* Decades later Tiny wrote, "I have been doubly blessed in this regard, having about a dozen real friends, the kind you treasure all your life."

During Tiny's first few weeks at North American (NA) he made the acquaintance of two men who were destined to become lifelong friends, George Belcher and Charles (Chuck) Shamp. George, a good old boy from Arkansas, never got angry and always stood with his friends. Chuck, too, was an even tempered gentle person who never got upset...nor in a hurry!

With a new job, a new bride and new friends, Tiny could not have been happier, with one exception. Buster did not seem very time conscious. Being on time was of little or no concern to him. On most mornings they had to run from the parking lot to punch the time clock, or be late...and some mornings they were not able to punch in on time. Tiny promised himself then that if he ever could afford a car, he would never be late, not for anything.

Assemblers at NA were classified as "A", "B", and "C". Tiny's hourly rate of $1.10 placed him at the top of the "C", meaning that unless he qualified for a change in classification, there would be no pay increases.

In December the company added a 2nd shift, and the supervisor of the new shift was asking for volunteers. Working night shift did not appeal to most men. However, when Tiny was offered the classification upgrade and a raise to $1.25 per hour, he was motivated. Tiny felt pretty cocky to have advanced so rapidly after only 4 months with the company.

Alieta became pregnant soon after marrying Tiny, prompting the couple to search for larger living quarters. That brought them to Willowbrook Ave. where they rented a three-room apartment from Malden and Anniel Bishop for $50 per month (double the rent they had been accustomed to paying). In the meantime, Alieta's parents had moved to California. A builder, her father erected a nice home in Imperial Beach, near San Diego.

May 29, 1949, John Andrew Gillum made his debut. Named for John Joseph Phillips (Alieta's father) and Andrew Jackson Gilliam (Tiny's father), Johnny-Boy was a healthy, active, blue-eyed blonde, and a bundle of happiness. Tiny continually marveled at having survived such a hectic life to experience such joy!

With increased rent and expense of a new baby, Tiny and his wife were unable to save any money. Still without a car, they did their shopping by taking Johnny in his stroller to the market. Returning, Tiny carried Johnny while Alieta pushed the stroller which contained their week's supply of groceries. Fortunately, the market was only 3 blocks away.

After Johnny arrived the family saw much more of Alieta's parents. If relations with them had improved (as, seemingly, they had), Tiny only had Johnny to thank for that. Shortly after the couple married, Tiny began calling Alieta May "Alex" because he saw in her a remarkable resemblance to Alexis Smith, the actress. With Alex and Johnny, his life was complete. Finding more to life than beer, girls, and job hopping, Tiny had become a "family man".

On November 30, 1949, Tiny received his first lesson on the perils of the aircraft industry. Due to cutbacks in the federal budget, NA contracts were affected, necessitating a major layoff. Buster and Tiny, being low on the seniority totem pole, were among those receiving the bad news. This was a very difficult time for Tiny because he really liked his job, and truly believed the job would last forever.

When any major manufacturer such as NA has to slow down, their suppliers are affected, making employment hard to find anywhere. Tiny signed up for unemployment benefits, and quickly discovered, that too was a waiting game. First there was the automatic 1-week waiting period, and then deductions for any vacation or separation pay received at time of layoff. Recipients had to report (meaning show up and wait) weekly. After 3 or 4 weeks of waiting, Tiny asked, "How much longer?"

The interviewer, who apparently thought he was being cute, said, "Don't worry. It's retroactive, and the longer you wait, the more you get when the time comes", as if unemployment were some kind of bonus plan. That was not the answer Tiny was looking for, nor an attitude he could deal with. Grabbing him by his necktie, Tiny sternly suggested the interviewer let him talk to someone with some brains, if he wanted to keep his teeth. That could have cost Tiny dearly; but, the interviewer pointing to his supervisor nearby convinced Tiny to turn him loose. Tiny was called back to work before receiving any benefits, leaving him with ill feelings about the system.

Canvassing for work took Tiny and Alex all over, including Orange County, south of Los Angeles. They applied for anything and everything, including the job of lighting smudge pots in the vast orange groves then so abundant in Orange County. During the Christmas holiday season they tried their hand at hosting "toy parties". With that work based on a commission plan, they discovered their out of pocket expenses were greater than the income they received. Consequently, the young couple experienced a lean Christmas spent with Alex's parents in Imperial Beach. Tiny and Alex had no money in their household but they did have their health and Johnny and were with family. Thus, they made the best of what could have been a much worse situation.

Tiny's best remembrance of that Christmas was the "recall notice" waiting for him on their return trip from

Imperial Beach. Good as the news was, there was some bad news attached...He would have to accept a downgrade to his original "C" classification and an attendant cut in pay. Even at that, the offer was good news, as working is a lot better than the alternative.

A few days later Tiny reported to the Long Beach plant as a rivet bucket. Buster was called back at the same time, but he returned to the plant at Downey. Bucking rivets inside an airplane wing section was a new experience for Tiny. Even with earplugs provided by the company, the noise was deafening. However, having been penniless at Christmas sobered him. He was working, and not about to complain. Perhaps that resolve affected Tiny's performance and attitude, because in about 3 weeks, his "B" classification was restored, along with the 20 cents per hour pay he had forfeited.

In March Tiny was called back to the Downey facility and assigned to the same program he had been working the previous November. He arrived just as the department softball team was being formed, and was invited to try out for the team. Considering the number of supervisory personnel there for the tryouts, Tiny figured his chances were about on a par with a snowball in hell! Moreover, the man who was organizing (and would manage the team) was a lowly peon like Tiny. Tiny figured the organizer would cotton to management for "points", but he was wrong. The team manager was only interested in building a group of what he thought were the best applicants, politics be damned. Tiny's competitors for 3rd base were a supervisor and a lead man. He got the starting assignment much to his surprise.

The Downey facility had a cafeteria, but most of the employees in Tiny's area were "brown baggers". Normally, employees gathered in groups to swap war stories, brag on their children, and gulp down bologna sandwiches. Some were automobile buffs, while some had other interests to discuss while eating lunch. Tiny remembered two men who would talk about nothing but cars throughout the lunch period every day of the week. Another fellow, who seemed to be a little more conversant on a variety of subjects, challenged them one day asking, "Why don't you guys talk about something that has a little more culture?"

One of the car buffs asked, "Like what?"

The more cultured gentleman suggested, "Like Beethoven, that's what."

The car buff, without hesitation, replied, "What kind of car did he drive?

Many of the employees were veterans of WWII. Some belonged to one of the military reserve units...Army, Navy, Air Force, etc., called "weekend warriors". They spent one weekend per month practicing their specialties, for which they were paid in accordance to their rank. Once, an Air National Guard member almost had Tiny convinced that the "weekend warriors" was a good way to supplement income. Invited to listen to a recruiter, Tiny told him he would think about joining and let him know on Monday. The so called "police action" in Korea flared up that Saturday. That made saying "no, thanks" to the recruiter easy for Tiny on Monday. Had he accepted the recruiter's offer, Tiny would have been activated for duty a few weeks later.

Even without the extra income, Tiny and Alex managed to make two major purchases in 1950: their first television set, a 12-inch black and white; and, a 1941 Chevrolet. They bought the car from Bob Loughland's father, who had purchased the car new, and had taken excellent car of the vehicle. The $300 price, even then, was a bargain. They had to borrow the money, which gave them some concern; but, after lots of thought, they decided to go ahead with the purchase. Having a car would allow them to do things with Johnny that, until then, was impossible.

Also about 1950 Tiny's friend Buster met a nice lady named Pearl, who had a lovely young daughter, Christine. Before too long romance bloomed, and Buster and Pearl were talking marriage. Unfortunately, Pearl's divorce was not final, but this would not stop them. They decided to run for the border, to Tijuana where they could be married immediately. Alex and Tiny went along and served as their witnesses. Although California may not have recognized a

Mexican marriage, Buster, Pearl, and Christine were satisfied with the marriage.

Buster had contacted rheumatic fever while in the Navy. That brought on a problem with a mitral valve in his heart. In time the condition began to plague him severely. One evening Pearl called, saying Buster was in great pain. They drove him to the Veteran's Administration Hospital in Long Beach immediately. At that time open heart surgery was still somewhat experimental, but Buster had no other option. Clearly, he would be dead within a few hours without corrective surgery. Tiny could not commend the Veteran's Administration enough. No time was wasted, and no expense (on their part) was spared. Buster was back to work in what seemed a very short time, considering the complexity of the surgery they performed. They were told that Buck was 1 of about 5 patients on which this type of surgery had been performed up until that time.

The AJ-1 contract was nearing completion by then, and the follow-up portion of the program was to be performed at the company's new Columbus, Ohio division. Many layoffs resulted because only "key" personnel were being transferred to Ohio. Buster's classification was not affected, and he remained on his current job. George Belcher and Chuck Shamp had previously transferred to the Los Angeles division, so they were not affected. Nor was Tiny, other than being transferred to the T-28 program, a trainer they were building for the Air Force.

Tiny was assigned to assist an "A" assembler in the engine cowling section. After about 3 months, he had to have emergency surgery that would keep him out for about 6 weeks. Tiny thought he was the likely candidate to move up, but was shocked to be told another man would be taking over for the fellow who was going on medical leave of absence. The proverbial straw was Tiny would be expected to train the new guy. This was 1 of the 2 times Tiny seriously considered leaving NA. To be designated as an assistant, then to be expected to train the one who would, in effect, be Tiny's boss, was beyond credibility. This, in no way, would he accept.

One more time Tiny decided he had less to lose by speaking up than by pouting. He informed the foreman that unless he was given a promotion to the job he was expected to train someone to do; he would be leaving at the end of the week. That conversation occurred on Monday. On Wednesday, Tiny was given a notice of upgrade in classification, but without a pay raise. He handed the notification back to the foreman, and told him that he could not accept the change without a raise. The foreman had the paperwork modified to include a raise in Tiny's hourly wage.

Tiny's friend, Bob Loughland, built a new home on the east side of Compton, and offered to rent his previous home to the Gillum family at $50 a month, exactly what they were then paying for a three-bedroom apartment. Tiny and his wife gave notice to the Bishops, and soon were settled in at 315 West Raymond Street. For the first time, they had an entire house with two doors, front and back, for their use only—plus a car and a TV set. Tiny really thought they were about as far uptown as they could hope to get. They were very proud of themselves, and what they had accomplished in the past year.

Alex and Tiny knew Christmas of 1950 would be much better than Christmas, 1949. Their euphoria was not to last beyond the coming spring. On April 9, 1951, the AJ-1 modification program ended. The vagaries of the aircraft industry are such that one must learn to roll with the profession's "ups" and "downs", and feel lucky if the ups outnumber the downs.

On termination of the AJ-1 program, several in Tiny's classification became surplus. Tiny was bumped from his job by an employee with more seniority, and given the option of night shift or layoff. Once again Tiny felt something is better than nothing, so he accepted the transfer to 2nd shift. About 6 weeks later Tiny was placed on open transfer again, meaning his job was once more in jeopardy. This time the decision was much more difficult. His options were layoff or transfer to the Los Angeles division. In addition to a long commute, Tiny would be working at the main plant where, according to rumor, the supervisors were intolerable, parking was impossible, and the working environment was intemperate. So vivid were these stories that Tiny seriously thought about accepting layoff! Fortunately, the interviewer had Tiny's interest at heart. Reasoning with Tiny, he urged him to accept the transfer, give the job a fair trial, and if he found conditions intolerable, then he could terminate. Also, he pointed out, Tiny was not receiving any reductions in pay. Tiny reported to the Los Angeles division May 28. Expecting the worst, he soon learned to pay no attention to rumors.

The drive was long as Tiny expected. Parking was not that bad and the supervisors were just like their brethren everywhere...ordinary working people with a job to do, and no better or worse than others he had known. By the end of October, Tiny was firmly settled in his new surroundings. Once again everything was going great but not for long.

On November 17 Tiny's world turned upside down. Working overtime on that never to be forgotten Saturday, Alex called to tell him that Johnny had swallowed some ant poison. While playing in the yard, he was swinging a stick and knocked the bottle of poison off a high window ledge where they had placed the bottle, thinking the location was out of Johnny's reach. Whether he loosened the bottle cap, or found the cap loose, they would never know.

Alex said that when she found Johnny, he had signs of the poison around his mouth. A neighbor drove him and Alex to an emergency hospital where they pumped his stomach, and released him. Tiny left work immediately. Alex and Johnny had already gotten back home when he arrived. Not satisfied that more serious harm had not been done, Tiny and Alex drove Johnny to Harbor General Hospital where there was a poison center and where, they hoped, Johnny would get the care they felt he so terribly needed. While sitting in a small cubicle out of sight from the nurses, Tiny overheard one say, "It looks like his chances are very slim."

Johnny passed at 9:55 a.m. the next day, Sunday, November 18, 1951. The doctors said he died from kidney failure. Johnny's death was a tremendous blow. He, not unlike the child of any mother or father, was more precious than life itself.

Tiny kept asking himself, *Why not me? I was the one who lived the rowdy, hell bent life. I was the one who never expected to live beyond 30. I was the one who never cared that much for life, until Johnny came along. Why Johnny? Why?* Tiny and Alex buried Johnny at Roosevelt Memorial Park in Gardena, not far from where Cliff and Norma would buy a house less than 2 years later.

"Goodbye, Johnny!"
5/29/49-11/18/51

Alex and many others expected Tiny to turn to the bottle after Johnny's death. In truth, Tiny surprised himself that he didn't. Drinking would have been an easy way of punishing himself. Instead, Alex and he turned to God, joining the First Baptist Church of Compton and accepting Christ as their personal Savior. Tiny's drinking days were over.

The void left by the loss of Johnny could not be filled, but Tiny truly believed the comfort of Christianity was his salvation. Having Buster and Pearl to lean on was vital to getting their lives reordered. In time wounds of the body heal; likewise, with the soul. The scars may remain, but the pain passes into oblivion. By year's end, Tiny and Alex were on their way to normalcy in their day-to-day lives.

Meanwhile on the job, Tiny had reached the top of his classification. Unless he received a promotion to lead man, there would be no more pay increases. He began looking for greener pastures, thinking that was his only option.

In early 1952, Tiny's brother Cliff, his wife Norma, and their daughter Karen Lynne moved to California, bringing Tiny and Cliff's mother with them. Cliff had no trouble finding work as a precision grinder due to his vast experience in that field at GM. Grinders were in great demand throughout the aircraft industry. On March 27 Cliff hired in at the Northrop Corporation in Hawthorne, California. He, Norma, and Karen

Lynne had no trouble adapting to California living, but their mother was not happy. She felt ill at ease, and truly missed Ashland and her lifelong friends. Her stay lasted no more than a couple of months.

"Looking for greener pastures", Tiny thought, *can be done without leaving "the ranch"*. The main thing he wanted was something that had promise of future advancement, and finding that with a new company and new employer could prove to be difficult. Within the NA complex, Tiny was sure, there had to be a job such as he had envisioned.

In August 1952, Tiny was offered a job in the inspection department. Asking for a release to transfer, Tiny's foreman turned him down. That was the second time he seriously considered leaving NA. Immediately filing an application for an inspection job at Northrop, he was accepted, but the offer was contingent on his termination of employment at NA. Tiny submitted his notice of termination the next day, and that is when Jim Long, inspection foreman, entered in. Puzzled that Tiny would forfeit his seniority with NA, Jim investigated. His intervention proved to be well worthwhile, as Tiny was transferred to the inspection department August 18 with a pay raise.

Tiny's first assignment in the inspection department was the F-86 wing line, with responsibilities for inspection of installations, wing mating, and landing gear operations. With previous experience limited to structure assembly, inspection was a revelation. The man Tiny was to replace was both expert in his field and a competent, patient teacher. Tiny's transition went smoothly. In a short time, Keith Mann (Tiny's mentor) moved to the final assembly line leaving Tiny to work alone. The other more experienced inspectors and the manufacturing personnel as well, treated Tiny with what he could only call "cordiality" from day 1. *Perhaps*, Tiny thought, *there might be resentment at one coming off a structure assembly line to inspect another's work in a more advanced area.* Tiny found the opposite to be true. The situation was as if they were saying, "You've paid your dues Gillum. God bless and good luck."

In October, 1952 Tiny had his turn calling on the VA Hospital in Long Beach for medical aid. He had contracted an eye infection, which they diagnosed as conjunctivitis (okay, pink eye, if you insist). His co-workers on the wing line saw the situation differently. They said he was straining his eyes too much trying to find fault in their work!

Other than his secondary experience with Buster's heart problem, seeking treatment for his conjunctivitis was Tiny's first brush with the United States government medical services. He was more than impressed with the manner in which he was treated, and even more so by the quality of the care he received. Those who would believe these services are mediocre or less than the best, take Tiny's word for it. Those tales, having no truth to them, are like the rumors that once almost cost Tiny his job. No effort was spared, and no civilian (commercial) hospital in America could provide more.

While on medical leave, Tiny's job performance came up for review. He came back to work to find notice of a pay raise. Five months later he was upgraded to final assembly inspector, where he joined his former mentor, Keith Mann.

At that time the United Automobile Workers (UAW) that represented hourly employees at NA called a strike. Memories of Tiny's strike experience in West Virginia struck terror in his mind. Although union membership was not mandatory and Tiny did not belong, he felt he should honor the picket line and joined the walkout. The strike was no more than a couple of days old when Tiny heard that others, including some union members were crossing the picket line and going back to work. *Rumors*, Tiny thought, so he sat out a week before going back in to see with his own eyes. The situation was as if there had never been a strike! Even the union steward was back at work. Tiny never missed another day.

Surprised again, when Tiny returned from his self-imposed strike, he learned he had been promoted to lead man, and would be responsible for a crew of inspectors on the fuselage line. This too resulted in another tidy pay raise.

On the fuselage line Tiny met two other gentlemen whom he would learn to call "honored friend": John Harris and Don Shearer. John was inspection lead man for the electrical group. Don was one of the inspectors Tiny had inherited in his new assignment.

The next 3 years were eventful in terms of progress at work, and in terms of deterioration of family life. Alex and Tiny were growing apart. The once great mutual satisfaction between them no longer existed in what the couple did or planned together. Some said Johnny's death was part of the split; Tiny could not accept that. Both he and Alex loved Johnny. His loss affected them both. That was true; but, Tiny didn't believe his demise was the problem. *Rather*, Tiny thought, *Alex's parents had been right all along. They were too young and too immature.*

Over the years as both Alex and Tiny matured, they did so at different levels, to different degrees, and became different people. By the summer of 1955, concluding there was no future, Tiny moved out taking only his personal belongings and his "work car", a 1947 Plymouth. He left her all the furnishings and a 1950 Ford. He also agreed to assume responsibility for their outstanding obligations. Their parting was friendly with no haggling over the terms of a financial settlement.

In August Alex hired a lawyer and divorce proceedings were soon underway. In spite of Alex's and Tiny's earlier agreement, her lawyer tried to make Tiny liable for things that were none of his concern. The lawyer wanted Tiny to agree to things that were not in his and Alex's original agreement. When Tiny balked at the lawyer's requests, he threatened Tiny with jail. At which Tiny responded by telling him that would be fine; but, in that case, he and his client would get nothing. Then Tiny walked out! Tiny chose not to appear at the hearing. The divorce was granted on the terms to which Alex and he originally agreed.

Then they began the 1-year wait then required by California law. Although never expressed, Tiny probably came away from marriage feeling a combination of rage, relief, and resolve: rage at himself for letting what once had been utopia slip from his fingers; relief from all the stress the marriage had become; and resolve that it would "never happen again". Tiny's solace became his work, the one place and one thing that let him escape from himself. He convinced himself there would be no woman in his life and, just to make sure, he created a list of prerequisites that he thought would be impossible to achieve.

First and foremost, Tiny would have to solve his own financial crisis. That alone would make future courtship or marriage impossible. Further, Tiny told himself, God would have to recreate Eve. There simply could be no other woman alive suitable for Tiny. Then one day he met Ruth! God, in His infinite wisdom, had recreated Eve long before, and called her "Ruth". Then, as if to show Tiny who was boss, He exposed her to Tiny's view.

At that time Ruth was the mother of three teenage children (which Tiny found hard to believe), in the process of divorce, and irresistible to Tiny. Because both Ruth and Tiny had yet to receive final divorce papers, coupled with the fact that part of Tiny's personal list of prerequisites (to resolve his financial problems) remained, they had time to get to know each other better. Although, Tiny said he could have told anyone the first moment he met Ruth, he knew she would one day be his bride.

Terms of Ruth's and Tiny's respective divorces left them with debts to pay, leaving little cash for entertainment. Between Pinochle games with friends and VFW dances with Cliff and Norma, they made it from day to day. However, they had times were they used their Sears charge card for cigarettes and other things for which they had no cash. Although Tiny's divorce became final in August, 1956, they had to wait until October for Ruth's divorce to become final. About this time, NA opened a plant in Fresno, California for the modification of the F-86 fighter. Thinking this might be an opportunity for Ruth and Tiny, and her children to relocate and start life over in a new environment, Tiny applied for a transfer. After a few weeks his transfer was approved, effective November 26. Ruth's request was denied because there were no openings in her classification. Thus, they planned on her terminating after Tiny was settled in Fresno.

Meanwhile, she and the children would stay behind until Tiny found a place to live.

Housing at that time was plentiful in Fresno. Tiny had no problem locating a three-bedroom home, which was purchased on the G.I. Bill, nothing down and very low interest. Payments were set at $75 per month until escrow closed, at which time a permanent monthly payment would be established.

On December 8 with the help of their good friend, John Harris, they loaded their belongings on a rented truck and headed for Fresno. By then Ruth's divorce was final. Two days later, December 10, 1956 Tiny and Ruth married at the Fresno County Court House, with one of the employees serving as witness. They were then a genuine family. Ruth's children, Carole Ruth (then 17), James Peter (then 16), and Michael Charles, nicknamed "Biff" (then 13) couldn't have meant more to Tiny if he had been their natural father. With 2 weeks still remaining of Tiny's vacation time, they decided to take a trip to Michigan, as a family, and call the trip their honeymoon. Prior to moving to Fresno, Tiny had traded his old '47 Plymouth in on a 1953 Chevrolet. This gave Tiny more confidence that they would be able to make the trip without incidence.

December 17 the new family of five with a mountain of luggage began their trek to Port Huron, where Ruth's father, sister, and one brother still resided. Other than being cramped for space, and Tiny's reservations about meeting Ruth's family, they were moving along pretty well until Murphy's Law caught up with them.

On Sunday just east of Flagstaff, Arizona, the transmission shifted into low gear without provocation. Nothing Tiny did made any difference. Discovering that Gallup, Mexico was closer than returning to Flagstaff, he drove the next 50 miles in low gear. Being Sunday, nothing was open so they rented a nearby motel for the night, hoping that Monday morning they would be on their way again. Alas, Murphy's Law never sleeps.

Limping into a Chevrolet dealer Monday, they learned there was but one man in Gallup called a transmission mechanic. He worked for a local Ford dealer and did transmission repairs for everyone in town! There was one little catch...he had just left town for a 2-week vacation!

With old Murphy working overtime, the Gillum family exercised their only alternative...driving another 75 miles in low gear to Grants, New Mexico. Somehow the family reached Grants before the Chevrolet dealer closed, and learned that they would have to have a rebuilt transmission installed because the high band in theirs was shot.

Naturally, Murphy decreed the transmission would have to be ordered from Albuquerque, which meant at least one more day of waiting. Tiny and his family resigned themselves to the wait, hoping that old Murphy would find other things to do and leave them alone for a while.

Next day as they patiently waited for the delivery truck to arrive from Albuquerque with the replacement transmission, they kept telling themselves they would be on their way again soon. But, once more, they learned that Murphy was still at work—the truck carrying their transmission had lost its transmission along the way, and another truck had to be dispatched to complete the mission!

After losing a total of 4 days (Sunday through Wednesday), Tiny and his family departed Grants $310 lighter than when they arrived...and that was the cost of the rebuilt transmission only. From Grants, they drove straight through to Port Huron, arriving there Christmas eve.

Beside the long wait, Tiny had one other memory of Grants, New Mexico: A wise old gentleman Tiny talked to there said it all when he gave Tiny the following unsolicited advice: "Son, automobiles are nothing but trouble, and as long as you own one, you will always have trouble." How right he was! In spite of annoyances and unexpected expenses, the trip in all other respects was a delight.

At one point Biff, sitting up front, and acting as navigator spotted a sign alongside Route 66 reading "Taters". The sign was obviously placed there by a local farmer seeking to sell surplus crop; but, Biff thought otherwise. After diligently searching the map for what seemed to be a very long time, he said, "I don't see the town of Taters anywhere on this map!"

At Port Huron, after meeting Ruth's family...her father, Joe, brother Bob and his wife Mary Lou...sister Catherin and her husband, Norv...Tiny realized his earlier concerns had been totally unfounded. Not knowing what their feelings might have been for Ruth's previous husband, Tiny feared they might resent his presence.

Ruth's family very quickly put Tiny's mind to rest, and convinced him the reservations and concerns were all in his head. Ruth's mother had passed away a few years before, so Tiny never had the pleasure of meeting her. Another brother, Harry (called Bud by the family) and his wife, Jeri lived in California's San Fernando Valley. Tiny had already met them prior to their relocation to Fresno. Prior to the Gillum family's arrival, Catherine had made arrangements (with Ruth and Tiny's knowledge and approval) to have the minister at their church perform a church wedding for them with Ruth's family in attendance.

After Tiny and his family departed Grants, they discovered they were still losing transmission fluid, necessitating frequent stops for replacing of fluid. Therefore, before leaving Port Huron on their return to California, Tiny drove to Flint, Michigan to register a complaint with General Motors. GM's public relations man sent Tiny to their service department where an inspection of the car revealed that the original problem had been a hole in the fuel line. Why this had not been discovered when the rebuilt transmission was installed was the mystery, and Tiny's concern. Realizing that a line costing a buck or two caused all their problems really made Tiny angry. He felt the hole should have been discovered and fixed at the time of the transmission installation. Tiny supposed the hole in the line could have been overlooked; but, the next statement Tiny heard really blew his mind! The employee in Flint told Tiny he would have to take his complaint to his district representative in Oakland, California. The fact that he had been put to so much expense for a transmission replacement and that he could have been out the cost of another one due to a dealer's negligence was too much. From that day forward Tiny avoided all General Motors products.

The trip back was uneventful until the family reached home. While checking his tires for damage that may have occurred during the trip, Tiny discovered big chunks of rubber missing from the sidewalls of all four recaps. This gave Tiny a few anxious moments realizing "what might have been", but then realizing a blowout had not occurred, he headed to Sears for new tires. Then he put the matter out of his mind. However, he could not help but think, *although Murphy got us on the transmission, he sure missed the boat on the tires!*

The Gillum family had not been home long when they learned that all the homes in their tract were in some kind of "escrow limbo". They had been told at the time of move in they would pay $75 per month until escrow closed in about 90 days. Word was out that the builder was having financial troubles and escrow would be delayed indefinitely, which meant they were only renting, not buying! They then learned that a group of homeowners in the tract had jointly hired a lawyer to protect their interests. They joined the action and paid their $50 retainer fee.

Ruth had applied for unemployment when they moved to Fresno, but her claim was denied because she had voluntarily terminated instead of being laid off. An appeal was filed, but nothing came of that. To help with expenses, she took a job with a local lawn sprinkler manufacturer. In time, with two paychecks, they managed to pay off the debts inherited with their divorces and move on with their lives.

With the approach of summer, Tiny was looking forward to some fishing in nearby mountain lakes and streams. Then the situation at work changed again! The company announced that the Fresno plant was being shut down due to a slowdown in business. Those hired at Fresno were given notice of layoff; while those like Tiny who had transferred there were given the option of layoff or return to the Los Angeles division.

For Tiny, there was no choice. He knew that accepting a layoff and remaining in Fresno would jeopardize any chance of being recalled. Unwilling to risk 9 years of seniority, he accepted the transfer.

Arrangements were made for the children to stay with relatives while John and Sugar Harris generously offered Tiny and Ruth temporary housing. With household goods loaded, the house key was turned over to their lawyer. Then they were on their way over the ridge route back to Southern California. Once there, they put their belongings in storage, and began the tedious search for an apartment.

In a week or two they were settled in Inglewood with the whole family together again. Reporting for work July 29, Tiny learned that his friend, the confirmed bachelor Chuck Shamp, had married a lovely lady named Louise, who would quickly mend those bachelor habits! Assigned to the position Tiny had before leaving for Fresno, circumstances seemed to be back to normal; but, at that time, the aircraft industry was in a volatile mood. Declines in government contracts forced many out of work, and those who remained were on a daily roller coaster ride. They all suffered through downgrades and cuts in wages. In the end, Tiny received his layoff notice.

With Tiny's layoff notice on the heels of Thanksgiving, they figured Christmas of 1959 might be another bleak one. However, that was not the case. Ruth got a job at Aircraft Tools in Inglewood. Tiny was fortunate to find work at the company of a friend, Mike Neushul. Mike was in the business of manufacturing hospital linen carts and food catering equipment.

In December, Ruth informed Tiny that he would be a father before the fall of 1960. The elation he felt knowing he would be a father again overshadowed any concerns about job, finances, or other matters. Times may not have been the best financially. However, they were holding their own and were able to slip away to one of their favorite haunts in Ojai frequently. Ruth, Biff, and Tiny sometimes accompanied by Cliff, Norma, and Lynne spent some relaxing and happy days there. Carole finished school while the family was still living in Fresno, and was working for Douglas Aircraft (now McDonnell Douglas). The boys, Pete and Biff, were attending Inglewood High School. They all shared the apartment for a time, but Carole moved to a place of her own and later married Daniel O'Connell.

On March 19, 1960 Carole and Daniel's first son, Jim, was born. Recalled to NA July 5, 1960, Tiny terminated his job with the Neushul Company. Ruth remained at Aircraft Tools beyond what should have been the cutoff date for pregnancy. The company, reluctant to see Ruth go, had to hire three employees to replace her. On August 7, 1960 Ruth gave birth to David Lee Gillum, which brought to a close Tiny's 1st dozen years in California with great hope and expectations for the future.

***

CHAPTER 7

California...
The 2nd Dozen Years

Soon after Dave was born Tiny and Ruth began looking for more suitable housing, seeking to buy instead of rent and using Tiny's G.I. Bill again. The suburban sprawl had not yet reached Orange County; the area was still quite rural with truck farms, orchards and the famous Irvine ranch as the area's most significant industries. Little did most suspect that homes then selling for $15,000 would 30 years later bring $275,000 or more. At that time $15,000 seemed expensive; today that amount would not even buy a vacant lot anywhere in Orange County. They looked at many areas in Orange and Los Angeles counties. A commute to and from Orange County on surface streets and country roads was then a 2-hour drive each way, so they passed on that area. After some time, and just when they were feeling hopeless, a friend of one of their friends bought a new home, and offered to sell them his previous residence in Torrance for $11,500. The price was right, but the house could not be bought on the G.I. Bill, meaning they would need quite a large sum of cash as a down payment.

Cash was something that was in short supply and long in demand at the time. Rather than force Tiny and Ruth into a compromising situation, the gentleman allowed the family to move in, and applied the rent towards a down payment...proving once again that faith in people is not always misplaced. Once Tiny and Ruth had paid enough rent to make the down payment, their rental agreement was converted to a purchasing agreement, with the monthly payments remaining the same as their monthly rent, plus interest. This was the break they needed! Their total monthly house payment including interest was $102.00 per month! Folks pay more than this amount for a 1-night stay in a motel today! To obtain the extra money needed, Tiny continued to work part time for his friend, Mike Neushul.

In Torrance, Tiny and Ruth met Shirley and Bill Ingles, who later became their very close friends. Ruth came to look upon Shirley as part of their extended family, almost like a daughter. They shared many interests, including crafts. Shirley had a passion for crafts involving feathers. One would often find them floating around her house when visiting. Their three sons, a little older than Dave, proved to be excellent playmates for him.

In February of 1961, Cliff and Norma became the proud parents of a daughter, Mary Frances (later nicknamed Mimi). She was a beautiful child, with long blonde tresses that Dave found irresistible. Careful as the parents were, Dave always managed a tug or two when she was near.

On April 9, 1961 Carole's second son, Daniel, was born. Pete graduated high school in June, 1961, and in October of that same year, married his high school sweetheart, Donna Jo Matthews. Shortly after their marriage, in November, he enlisted in the United States Air Force. They moved to Kansas where Pete was to be stationed.

In due time Dave found his land legs and with help from everything in the house he began walking. Biff stepped into the breach as our built-in babysitter, without being asked. He also helped with the chores an infant imposes…from feeding to changing and everything in between…a most unusual young man.

Dave's favorite trick was emptying ashtrays, but he never bothered about where he emptied them. Ruth gave up smoking about then. Perhaps Dave's propensity for dumping ashtrays had something to do with her decision. Sometime later Tiny followed her lead; probably one of the really smart things he did in his lifetime.

While living in Torrance, Tiny and Ruth took up golf. They had played a small, somewhat rundown, course in Inglewood, but this was their first attempt at breaking par on a fairly decent course. One day soon after they became serious golfers, Ruth scored a birdie on a 3-par hole at the Alondra Park course where they played. She could have been heard in Philadelphia, had they been listening.

Cliff was laid off from Northrop in late 1960. His desires were to continue as a precision grinder, but found jobs very scarce in his field at the time. He later went to work for NA as a precision assembly inspector. Unsure whether he wanted to be an inspector at first, the position worked out quite well for him.

On August 4, 1962, Donna gave birth to James Patrick O'Connor. Annmarie was born November 28 the same year to Carole and Danny. This gave Tiny and Ruth a total of four grandchildren. Pete was unable to spend much time with "Jimmy" at first, as he was sent to Vietnam shortly after Jimmy was born. Pete's stint in Vietnam lasted approximately 1 year, but he was sent home for discharge just before the communist forces began their offensive, which relieved Tiny and Ruth's many concerns about him being there.

Work, since being recalled in July of 1950 was progressing very well. Soon after his return, Tiny was promoted to final inspection lead man with an attendant pay rate that made life a bit more comfortable. Even so, Tiny kept his part-time job with Mike Neushul. By 1963, the Apollo program was getting started, and in the summer, Tiny transferred to the company's Space and Information System Division in Downey, thinking such a move offered greater promise for his future.

President John F. Kennedy, prior to his assassination by Lee Harvey Oswald in November, 1963 had made a pledge: America would land a man on the moon during the 60's decade. This effort would require new sciences, new technologies, new materials, new assembly, and new inspection techniques. With hardware far more sophisticated than that of either the F-86 or F-100 aircraft, Tiny expected the change to be an exciting experience. He was surprised, though, to find the inspection techniques similar to that of high-tech aircraft and with far less pressure for immediacy. The emphasis on quality so far exceeded the demand for speed and production that Tiny sometimes found the routine downright boring, which shocked him.

The Saturn S-2 was the second state of the Apollo "stack" and housed five powerful engines that would be used to propel the Command Module into orbit. The S-2 was being manufactured at the division's Seal Beach facility, where Tiny eventually hoped to work.

In the nearby vicinity to the Seal Beach facility a sizable housing boom was underway. Since the prices had not yet escalated into the sub-stratosphere, Tiny contacted his friend George Belcher, who was an inspection lead man at Seal Beach, to ask him to watch for any openings that might occur. Before long George called Tiny to say there was an opening in his area. Tiny submitted a transfer request, which was approved. He reported to the Seal Beach facility November 1, 1964.

In December of 1964, Tiny and Ruth sold their house in Torrance and bought a new place in Garden Grove, only 5 miles from the Seal Beach plant. Dave, who was then just past 4, was the only one of the children to accompany them on the move. Biff had graduated from Narbonne High School in Torrance and had taken a position with the post office in Long Beach where he also was living. Too young to grasp the word "geography", much less its meaning, Dave kept asking, "When are we going to move back to California?"

Tiny found duties in his new assignment varied and interesting. Approached about a desk job in September of 1965, Tiny hesitated. John Hearn, an inspector whom Tiny had worked with in Los Angeles was then a supervisor in Technical Integration (one of many sections of the Quality Assurance organization). The Technical Integration charter included the accumulation of test and fabrication records that later became a part of the S-2 vehicle delivery requirements.

Informed the change would carry a tidy increase in pay made the decision much easier to make. Even then Tiny had moments of doubt when he heard a rumor suggesting he would be assigned to Downey after the transfer became effective. Not anxious to trade a 10 mile round trip (Garden Grove to Seal Beach) for one of almost 40 miles (Garden Grove to Downey), Tiny confronted John Hearn with what he had heard. John assured Tiny the rumor was not true and sent him to see the supervisor at Seal Beach under whom he would be working. That's when Tiny met Emmett Charles Edwards.

Emmett was a bright young man just under 30 and, as Tiny later would learn, a man with a mind of his own! When Tiny approached Emmett, he regarded Tiny's doubt with less than what he thought was satisfactory concern, prompting him to ask for more specifics. Emmett told him he would be doing a variety of jobs at Seal Beach, Downey, and Santa Susana (about 60 miles northeast of Seal Beach). Asked where Tiny's "base" of operations would be, Emmett said, "You'll be working in various locations."

Tiny was ready to reject the offer, but not before he asked Emmett where he would report each day to commence his typical work day. His reply, "Seal Beach", was what Tiny wanted to hear. Later that day, Tiny called John and told him to process the paperwork.

October 2, 1965 Pete and Donna presented Tiny and Ruth with their fifth grandchild, a beautiful little girl. She was christened Sheri.

October 10, 1965 Tiny reported for his new assignment with some reservations about his earlier conversation with Emmett. Although the primary function of technical integration was the accumulation of vehicle acceptance and delivery date, several other records management tasks were involved. Accumulated data were presented to the customers, the National Aeronautics and Space Administration (NASA), in the form of an Acceptance Data Package (ADP) for review and approval. Upon approval, the ADP became part of the vehicle delivery to the test site. Preparation of the ADP and subsequent review with NASA would be Tiny's responsibility. His previous duties as an inspector required daily contact with NASA personnel. This made Tiny a definite asset to the technical integration organization because he had, long ago, established an excellent rapport with NASA employees.

During the time the Seal Beach group was in the first stages of organization, the data accumulation effort had been performed by Downey personnel. When the first elements of data were brought to Seal Beach for review, the NASA resident manager refused to conduct the review. He informed Emmett there would be no review until Tiny had personally performed a review and assured him the data was correct!

In 1966 Tiny and Ruth's extended family grew once again. Their sixth grandchild Chris, third child of Carole and Danny, was born January 21 that year. Both Pete and Carole and their families lived only a short distance from Tiny and Ruth's house on Acacia Avenue. Thus, Ruth had and took advantage of every opportunity to spoil the grandchildren.

While Ruth spoiled the grandchildren and continued to care for Dave, Tiny continued to develop his friendships at work. One of the employees who already reported to Emmett when Tiny transferred in was Bob Sherohman. He also was a former inspector, well suited for that type of work. He knew both inspection and manufacturing systems thoroughly, which made him an excellent auditor of the records. Bob and Tiny became very good friends, working together for most of the next 20 years.

Emmett and Tiny's relationship grew into an everlasting friendship, bridging the gap between work and personal lives. Emmett once told Tiny that at the time of their first meeting his urge was to tell Tiny to "get lost"; but, his boss had previously told him to make sure all Tiny's questions were answered to Tiny's satisfaction. Except for that admonition, Emmett and Tiny might never have had the opportunity to become the good friends they were for many years, which Tiny felt would have been his own loss!

By April, 1967 the Seal Beach facility had become a beehive of activity. The Technical Integration organization was fully staffed and consisted of three groups: Records Management, Systems Configuration, and ADP Compilation. After being promoted to supervisor April 2, 1967, Tiny was assigned the responsibility for the ADP Compilation group. Emmett, at his request, was transferred to Records Management in Downey. Frank Littlefield, a slow talking redheaded Texan, was supervisor of the Systems Configuration group. Their boss, Ed Earl, was a sophisticated individual that, initially, was very aloof and did not mingle too much with the employees. That soon changed once he began to understand the old hillbilly ways of Tiny!

In the short span of 18 months Tiny had progressed from a product analyst to supervisor—quite an accomplishment for an old country boy with no more than a 9th grade education. He kept waiting for someone to come along and say, "Wake up boy! You've been dreaming."

With the added income from his most recent promotion, Tiny was able to give up the part-time job to spend more time with Ruth and Dave. This made Ruth happy, but Dave? That was a different story! He wasn't sure he liked his dad being home so much. He begged Tiny to go back to work for Mike Neushul, so he would have his momma to himself once more. She read to him, and he liked that. With Tiny around she had less time to read to Dave. He resented that (not that Tiny could blame him). Those circumstances weren't long in lasting.

The S-2 program was accelerated to make every effort to meet President Kennedy's goal of putting a man on the moon in the 1960's decade. Doing so required long hours and hard work for everyone involved, including Tiny. At times, he spent as much as 36 consecutive hours on the job. Then, after no more than a "break" for shower and shave, went back to work. For Tiny and America, this was an exciting time, a time in which historical events piled one upon the other, it seemed, day by day, week by week. This was an era in which mankind's technology exceeded 2 centuries or more.

Tiny was very fortunate to have top quality people on his staff, men who knew their job and who took pride in doing things well. Two group leaders stood out: Bob Claytor and Jack White. *They were capable of miracles*, Tiny thought, *when they needed to make things happen on time!* Jack from Urbana, Ohio, one of the newer members of the group, transferred from Logistics.

Bob, another Buckeye, was a former inspector Tiny had known previously. Off the job, they became friends and along with Bob and his wife, Marylyn, Tiny and Ruth developed some bad habits. They played Pinochle with the couple. The habit of eating during the games got them into trouble, and began Tiny's "battle with the bulge", which did not end there.

The first two completed S-2 stages, designated S-2F and S-2T, were used for testing at the Mississippi Test Facility (MTF) near Long Beach, Mississippi. During one test, the S-2T exploded, triggering an investigation by NASA at Downey, Seal Beach, and MTF. Word reached Tiny about 2 a.m. with instructions to report to work immediately.

Records documenting manufacture and test of the vehicle were impounded until a government audit team arrived. Within 48 hours Government Accounting Office (GAO) personnel arrived like a swarm of locusts! They had questions about everything, including their own questions. In the end, no particular group or individual was found responsible. The explosion was determined to have been accidental, and beyond any human ability to foresee.

For about a week, the work atmosphere was tense with nobody making jokes about what had occurred. Weekly status meetings were conducted during the fabrication and testing of the vehicle. NA staff chaired the meetings with NASA personnel in attendance. Chairing the meetings was Tiny's responsibility. Not one who enjoyed standing in front of an audience to air his thoughts, Tiny was taken out of his comfort zone with this new experience. Briefing charts depicting percentage of completion for various data items, plus estimated completion dates, were required to be presented. Tiny stumbled through the first of these meetings; but, soon they became routine.

When serial 001 of the flight configuration was delivered to MTF, Tiny was asked to participate in a joint review of the accompanying data. This would require Tiny to fly. He'd always thought, *when God gives me wings, I'll fly!* This was something Tiny did not care a lot about doing, even with the help of man's inventions; but, orders were orders! The highlight of the trip was a visit to New Orleans on a sightseeing tour (his 1st time there), which he did enjoy very much. Fortunately for Tiny, with his fear of flying, that was the last time he was called upon to make such a journey for the company.

With his discomfort in flying, over the years Tiny avoided doing so as much as possible. Anytime Tiny would travel to visit family in Kentucky or Michigan, he would drive. When he became too old to drive, others drove him or he rode the train.

Around the time Tiny was working with NASA to help put a man on the moon, his brother Cliff transferred into Technical Integration from the Quality Planning group. He worked at the Compton facility in the Ground Support Equipment (GSE) section. Cliff's duties were similar to those of Tiny's group of technicians but for the various GSE items that supported vehicle handling, test operations, and shipping.

S-2 vehicles were moved by a special transporter from the Seal Beach facility to a loading dock, where they were put aboard a barge for the trip to MTF. The route traveling from plant to dock passed an intermediate school. Tiny always called the principal's office on the day prior to the scheduled event with an approximation of the time when one of these mammoth pieces of hardware would be passing. Anyone who has not seen one of these vehicles could not imagine the faces of wonder on the youngsters that Tiny saw lined up to see the view.

On December 21, 1968 Saturn S-2 Serial 003 propelled Apollo Spacecraft into orbit on a 7-day mission to orbit the moon. This was followed by two more lunar orbits in March and May of 1969. These missions were in preparation for man's first moon landing. On July 16, 1969, 6 months and 26 days after that first launch, Astronauts Neil Armstrong, Michael Collins, and Edwin Aldrin achieved lunar orbit aboard Spacecraft 107. A few hours later Neil Armstrong, under the watchful eye of the world, gave America and its people a moment of triumph, one of which John F. Kennedy would have been equally proud, when he made his now famous proclamation of "A giant step for mankind". By the end of 1969 the S-2 program was winding down. While Tiny and others were putting the finishing touches to the 15th and last flight stage, many changes were being made within the organization.

As is common during periods of change, rumors began to fly. One circulating rumor indicated that NA was merging with an as yet unnamed company and that, in turn, gave rise to the usual barrage of wisecracks. One of the lots, and the most humorous, stated that the company would be merging with Mothers Oats and Smucker's Jams, which would then result in the company being known as "North American Mother Smucker's".

In the end, NA merged with Rockwell Tools and became known as North American Rockwell (NAR). Following the S-2 phase out, thousands of workers became surplus and were laid off or downgraded. Tiny was stripped of his supervisor rating and assigned a staff position (with no loss of pay). Study contracts for the forthcoming Space Shuttle had been awarded by NASA, and NAR was one of those being considered for the role of prime contractor. To be confident experienced employees would be available, a skills retention list was compiled. Emmett, Bob, Jack, and Tiny were relieved to find their names on the list. Cliff also made the list in his GSE area. While waiting for the awarding of the Space Shuttle contract, employees, including Tiny, occupied themselves with tasks ranging from audits to test site support and new business proposals. This was not the most exciting time for Tiny; but, he had no responsibilities for other personnel, which allowed him to work under considerably less tension. Honestly, like others, Tiny was thankful to still have a job during such indecisive times.

Although the aerospace industry was enduring another slow time, the Rockwell side was prospering. The automotive supply and tool producing divisions were flourishing. The company also was acquiring many smaller companies (some of which were foreign based). With expanded foreign trade, NAR came to be known as Rockwell International (RI).

During the next couple of years the Apollo program was in the public limelight with more moon landings. As these landings became somewhat commonplace, public interest declined. The men and women involved with these programs were very much unlike the general public and for good reasons. Tiny and others in the field watched in total fascination and breathed an audible sigh of relief every time one of those powerful S-2 engines ignited to propel another command module into space.

Back on the home front, Tiny's son Dave turned 11 years old August 7, 1971. Until then, Dave had expressed little interest in baseball; although, Tiny prayed for the day he would do so. Tiny had long since resolved to not push Dave, but let him know very clearly that he only needed to "let me know" when and if he decided to give it a go. At that point Tiny would sign Dave up for the West Garden Grove Little League. To Tiny's surprise and delight, Dave elected to give baseball a try. With enormous pride and pleasure, Tiny began preparing Dave for the tryouts, scheduled to begin in early January of 1972.

An agile youngster, neither clumsy nor awkward, Dave did very well at the tryouts; well enough, in fact, that he was drafted by the Pirates of the Major division. Little

League majors are the highest level of competition, other than the Senior and Big League division. Normally the majors are open only to those who have played in the various minor divisions earlier. The coach was surprised to learn Dave had no previous playing experience but still allowed him to attend the pre-season practice sessions.

When the time for cuts came, the coach went to Tiny and said he was cutting Dave, and that Dave would be playing the next lower division, the Minor "A". The "A" division was composed of mostly 10 and 11 year olds, with a few 12 year olds interspersed. Tiny was not unhappy with the coach's decision, because he knew that Dave would be better off at the lower level his 1st year. Had he made the Pirate's team, he would have played very little anyway, due to the number of returning team members from the previous year's team. Tiny was just thrilled to know Dave would be playing, and that Dave himself had made the choice to do so.

The work scene in the meantime had been going through more drastic changes. Cal Groves, Director of Quality Assurance (and Tiny's boss) had accepted an offer to transfer to the newly formed Missile Systems Division (MSD) in Columbus, Ohio. His objective was to establish a Quality Assurance organization in support of the new Condor Missile contract recently awarded by the Navy. Prior to his departure, Cal discussed the possibility of having Emmett and Tiny join him in this undertaking. The proposition had benefits, but would have to be weighed on balance. Emmett displayed much more enthusiasm than Tiny, if only because Tiny remembered how cold and miserable the winters can get in that neck of the woods. Having Ruth closer to her family would be nice. Additionally, the family would be closer to Ashland. Tiny and Ruth also considered whether they might want to settle there in retirement, which was no more than 10 years away. These were viable considerations, but there were others. One of these was that just as Dave would be finishing his 1st year of Little League baseball, they would be leaving the area. This meant he would have to begin all over again the following year in totally different surroundings. Leaving friends at Dave's age is also a very traumatic experience for most children. The potential effect on Dave too had to be considered. Nothing would happen before the end of summer, so Tiny and Ruth had ample time to consider all options.

When the Minor "A" division conducted its draft in late February, Dave was drafted by the Orioles. At the time of signups, Tiny had been asked if he would be willing to help with coaching. Of course, he jumped at that opportunity! At that time Tiny met the man known affectionately as "the pride of Aransas Pass (Texas)", Harvey Langham, who also had a son on the Orioles. Dave's other coach, Cal Callaway, also was an Aransas Pass native. Like Dave, Harvey's son, Ron, was in his 1st year of play. Cal and wife Debbie's son, David, was not yet old enough to sign up.

In addition to Dave and Ron, several other members of the Orioles were short on experience, so this was to be a learning time for all, players and coaches alike. Thus, began the long, tiring, and tedious period of practice where the coaches would, hopefully, prepare the boys to play the various positions.

Dave, being tall and lanky, with long fingers, was a primary candidate for pitching. He could throw a baseball hard enough to penetrate a brick wall. Unfortunately, at first, he could seldom hit the wall! Remembering how Tiny had ruined his arm through lack of coaching, he asked to be Dave's coach and trainer.

After stepping off the regulation pitching distance for Little League (46 feet) in their backyard, Tiny and Dave began working on a daily basis. Tiny's first tactic was to slow Dave down a bit, and work on his control. Father and son developed a schedule of "simulated" innings to be pitched each day, beginning with no more than two.

Each day when Tiny arrived home from work, Dave pitched according to their schedule, gradually increasing the number of innings per day to six (the amount of innings in a Little League regulation game). He learned to throw a curve and a sinker. Tiny made absolute certain Dave used a downward motion when he released the ball. This was to assure there would be minimal elbow damage. After Dave had mastered these two pitches, they went to work on the knuckler. By mid-season, Dave was one of the better pitchers in the "A" division. Additionally, his control had improved 100%.

The Orioles did not set any records in that season, but they did play well at times and all the boys and coaches fully enjoyed the season. Ron Langham showed the most overall progress, going from a boy who didn't know how to hold a glove to a skillful fielder and good hitter. He and Dave each hit a home run during one game.

Meanwhile, in regards to work, Cal Groves had been assessing the situation in Columbus. In due time Emmett and Tiny received offers to transfer there. Emmett's offer would name him as Manager of the Quality Engineering department. Tiny's, although not including a promotion, did extend a satisfactory increase in pay. Then was the time for Tiny and Ruth to give the matter serious consideration. Taking Dave away from his new found interest in baseball (and his friends) was a major hurdle to overcome. Additionally, should they make the move, Ruth and Tiny having experienced Midwest winters in the Great Lakes basin knew what to expect. Dave, on the other hand, hardly knew what snow looked like! Moreover, when Ruth and Tiny grew up in that climate, neither of them had the comfort of forced air heating in the winter or air conditioning for the hot, muggy summers. By the time Ruth and Tiny made their decision, Emmett was already on the job in Ohio. Explaining the options, pro and con, to Dave, Ruth and Tiny realized later in hindsight, was too much pressure for a 12-year-old youngster who had never known anyplace outside Southern California. In the end Tiny decided to accept the job offer, notifying Emmett to start the ball rolling.

Tiny's reporting date was scheduled for August 14, 1972, leaving them about 30 days to sell the house and complete other arrangements for moving. Tiny planned to drive, leaving several days before Ruth and Dave. They would fly in after Tiny reached Columbus. Tiny and Ruth thought this, the end of Tiny's 2nd dozen years in California, would be the beginning of a new era in a new location. Well, at least, that's what they thought!

***

CHAPTER 8

A Prelude to Retirement

Tiny truly believed that uprooting his family in California to settle in Ohio was the proper move to make at the time. He did not know like so many other seemingly real situations in the past, the move was destined to fail.

The day Tiny arrived in Columbus was an ugly one. Angry clouds hung over the city. By the time he registered at the Howard Johnson Motel, heavy rains were falling. This was the first time Tiny had witnessed such a thunderstorm in years. He was just as frightened as when he was a boy in Kentucky! That was only the beginning.

Ruth and Dave arrived the next day. The day after their arrival, the Tiny and Ruth began their search for a place to live. They planned to rent for a while to give them time to study both the area and housing opportunities before buying. Some of the schools were on half-day sessions, which they did not favor. They wanted to learn more about services, facilities, and, just as important, the freeway layout. Their search for temporary housing ended on the north side of the city, where they would be close to the Outer Belt freeway, which Tiny would use daily in his commute to and from work. Shopping centers, restaurants, theatres, etc. also were conveniently nearby.

Tiny and Ruth rented what in that area is called a side-by-side (a duplex to others). However, a unique difference was the placement of two one-car garages between the apartments. This afforded a little more privacy than in the typical duplex.

Although Tiny's and his family's residence would be in the city of Columbus, Dave would be attending school in Westerville, about 10 miles to the northeast. This would later cause problems for him, but that was impossible to foresee. School bus service was available, but they opted to have Ruth drive him to school.

Tiny's 1st day at MSD was not very comfortable. Of course, old friends, Cal and Emmett, welcomed him with open arms but not so the others. Most of the Quality Engineering personnel had been transferred from the Columbus Aircraft division, with whom they shared facilities. Being from the old school of aircraft construction, these men were not accustomed to sophisticated missiles made from exotic materials. Moreover, they resented what they termed an invasion by "Space Cadets from California". Tiny could immediately feel the hostility. The embers of resentment were fanned into open flame when Emmett introduced Tiny as their new group leader!

Being a new division, MSD had no operating procedures. Previous to Tiny's arrival, a Navy quality team had conducted an audit and cited the organization for several infractions, one of which was the absence of a Quality Assurance Operating Manual. The director, Joe Halisky, was a former NASA quality resident at Seal Beach. He was a no-nonsense type who lived by the motto, "JUST DO IT!"

Joe called a meeting with Emmett and Tiny at 6 a.m. one morning, at which time he was adamant that such an operating manual would be "written, approved, and in operation within 90 days." This was Tiny's first major assignment, and major it was! Tiny suggested that they first needed a Division Standard Operating Manual that identified contractual requirements. Since there was none, writing a Quality Assurance Manual would be virtually impossible. Joe's reply was brief and to the point. He said, "I don't care. JUST DO IT!" Given authority to draw "what" and/or "who" was needed from "where" information could be found to complete the task, Tiny's first call went to Jack White, recently divorced and a native of the Columbus area (in

A Prelude to Retirement

addition to being just the right man with the skills needed), Tiny thought Jack might welcome the offer, which he did.

Emmett had previously brought in L. D. Bales and Chuck Creekmore from MTF to help bridge the gap between the "Air Crafters" and the "Space Cadets". With the addition of Jack, our team totaled six, which would help to even the odds, and allow them to "kick butts", if that's what circumstances required. The men in Tiny's group were eagerly expecting and eagerly waiting for him to fall on his fancy pants Space Cadet butt! None of them seemed to know the meaning of the word "procedures"; but, they were about to learn! Until Jack arrived, Tiny knew completing the job would be up to him, with one exception. One and only one man named Earl in the group seemed to be interested in what they were undertaking and offered his help.

Being unfamiliar with the task, about all Earl could do was legwork; but, he did a prestigious job of that! None of the manuals in use by other divisions would completely satisfy the Condor requirement. However, Tiny hoped with a little cutting and pasting, they might be able to use certain portions of those procedures. With help from Earl, Tiny first prepared a large chart identifying, by number and title, the procedures that would ultimately comprise the manual. The chart also provided spaces for entering the "scheduled" and "actual" completion dates of the various procedures. When that chart went up on the wall behind Tiny's conference table, the others began to take him more seriously!

Preparation plans called for coordination meetings with the various MSD organizations to solicit comments prior to release of individual procedures. The first meeting produced more arguments than comments. At the second meeting, only one man showed up! Tiny's choice of 5 p.m. for commencing the meetings might have had some effect on attendance. After that second meeting, Tiny decided the meetings were a waste of time. With no time to waste, he dispensed with any further meetings.

As each procedure was completed, Tiny wanted Cal Groves to sign off on what had been done before release. At first Cal displayed reservations about operating in this manner. When Tiny suggested to him that if he didn't want to lead, he had better follow, and get out of Tiny's way, Cal delayed the approval cycle no further. Tiny had no further problems after that confrontation.

As soon as Jack indicated acceptance of the job offer made to him, Tiny walked his paperwork through the system to expedite his arrival. With him soon at the desk behind Tiny, the ball really started rolling. With Jack's experience and assistance, even the most skeptical began to believe the Space Cadets actually did have a little knowledge, and that MSD would soon have a Quality Assurance Manual in operation. As typical, forms control assigned the upcoming manual a publication number. Soon thereafter, they asked how many binders and what color Tiny would want. With their concern being to get the manual together, no one had given any thought to any color scheme. To Tiny, what color the manual would be was the least of his worries. Thus, when asked looking at the color of his badge, Tiny said, Orange." Of course, the manual color was dubbed "MSD Orange".

The manual was completed and in use throughout Quality Assurance in the receiving, shipping, manufacturing, and testing departments well within Tiny's 90-day ultimatum. MSD did not have a Standard Operating Manual defining all requirements, but the employees in Quality Assurance had no problem knowing what to do!

Meanwhile, homesickness was taking a toll on Dave. Attending school at Westerville, Dave had not met any new friends in the area where the family lived. Most of the students with whom Dave went to school with lived in Westerville. He was not the only one missing friends or homesick for California. Emmett and his family were so unhappy that he was already seeking a transfer back "home" to California. Soon after the year's first snowfall, Emmett made connections in Downey, and was moving his family back to sunny California! His departure caused Tiny to have second thoughts also.

Even though Tiny could afford the forced air heating and the air conditioning that made indoor living more

A Prelude to Retirement

comfortable, he still had to face the cold and cope with the ice and snow going to and from work. He shuddered to think of the upcoming long hot summer, and the misery that would bring. Tiny's entire family had to deal with the elements in other facets of daily life. None of them liked the winter weather. On trips to the market, seeing the snow fall, Tiny found himself asking, "What in the hell am I doing here?"

    Shortly after settling in Columbus, Tiny bought Ruth a 1973 Plymouth Volare station wagon. The wagon was garaged requiring Tiny's old sedan to be parked outdoors at night. One morning Tiny awoke to what he thought was rain, only to discover (when he was ready to leave for work) what the locals called "freezy skid stuff", freezing rain or sleet, as referred to in Kentucky! The windshield covered with ice had to be cleaned. So, without thinking, Tiny grabbed the water hose. Big mistake! As soon as the water hit that glass, a solid sheet of ice formed! This incident taught Tiny a very valuable lesson: cover the windshield at night.

    Mexican food was one of the things Tiny and his family missed most about Southern California. Ohio had very fine Italian, Polish and Greek restaurants but few Mexican. One of Tiny's co-workers suggested a place about 20 miles away. Back in California, that was like next door. One evening Tiny and Ruth decided to try the restaurant, anticipating a real treat. What they found was a drag! Housed in the basement of an old rundown building in what can best be described as a dark alley, the place caused Tiny and Ruth serious misgivings. However, they decided they would at least give the place a try. They'd had better Mexican TV dinners!

    Early in 1973, Cal Groves received an ultimatum from his wife: Go back to California, or else. Tiny suspected Cal might have suffered only mild reluctance himself. The fact that he had talked Tiny into moving to Columbus, and was now contemplating bailing out, would not set too good with Tiny, Cal thought. Little did he know at the time, Tiny would have given anything to go with him. Another sobering thought entered Tiny's mind: *If Cal does leave, I will be the only original "Space Cadet" remaining, and among that bunch of air crafters, I won't stand a chance!*

Thoughts of returning to California were not unanimously appealing. Tiny and Ruth decided to say nothing to Dave, unless, or until they knew what would happen. From Ruth's point of view, Columbus was convenient to her family in nearby Michigan. Additionally, California had no overpowering attraction for her. Although Ashland too was close, the fact that they could visit there more often did not enter into Tiny's decision making whatsoever. Like Dave, Tiny was more than ready to head west, and back to real living! Knowing that both Dave and Tiny were unhappy, Ruth was willing, as usual, to go along with their desires.

Nothing regarding California had been resolved when the 1973 Easter school break arrived. Tiny and Ruth thought that would be a good time to visit Florida, tour the Kennedy Space Center, and take Dave to Disneyworld. A drive of just over 1,000 miles each way shouldn't have been a problem with a week's time in which to make the trip. What they failed to consider was the weather. They made the trip in blinding rain watching the windshield wipers, and seeing very little of the countryside as they traveled. At Orlando, the sky opened up with rains the likes of which Tiny had not seen only in New Guinea back in 1944. A day at Disneyworld in the rain was followed by one at the Kennedy Space Center, also in the rain but enjoyable. The weather showed no sign of clearing up, so they headed back to Ohio with a short stopover in Ashland to visit family on the way. The time Tiny and his family spent in Florida was much shorter than what they might have liked had the weather been nicer.

While in Ashland, Tiny and his family visited the home of his first cousin Marvin Owens (Uncle Harry and Aunt Earl's only child), known as "Smokey" to Tiny in earlier years. When in a conversation with Marvin, Tiny shared about his chance of being transferred back to California but that he hated to leave his mother since they hadn't been back East for too long. At that, Marvin replied, "Don't worry about her. I'll look out for her."

"I'd appreciate that," Tiny replied. "That makes me feel better."

Marvin lived up to his word too. Thereafter, every Thanksgiving, Christmas, and on other occasions Tiny's mother, as long as she was able, spent time with Marvin's family, along with her previously widowed sister, Earl. Marvin's willingness to care for Tiny's mother in her aging years strengthened the bond the two cousins had experienced as children. Thereafter, anytime Tiny was in the Ashland area, he always visited Marvin, even spending the night at his home in later years.

A few weeks later Cal Groves called Tiny with "good news" and "bad news". The good news, he said, was that he had a job for Tiny, but the bad news was he could not offer him a raise. Under the circumstances, Tiny told Cal both his statements were good news and that he was more than ready to start packing! Once more, Tiny and Ruth decided not to tell Dave until the offer was "in hand" with all parties in agreement. On that wonderful day that everything became official, Tiny went home where he and Ruth called Dave into the living room. Trying to remain calm and display no emotion, Tiny asked him if he would like to move back to California. Dave grinned so wide his ears almost fell off. He kept asking over and over, "Are you kidding?" Assured not, Dave ran through the house yelling, "We're going home to California!" Tiny doubted very much that he slept that night.

In time, which to Tiny seemed like an eternity, transfer documents were processed, including full relocation expenses, and enough time to wrap things up in Columbus. Tiny's report date at the Los Angeles Division was May 20, 1973. With about 4 months remaining on their lease, the landlord indicated he would not "hold them" to the terms of the lease. Considering that he would be obliged to rely on their sending monthly payments, and that Tiny and Ruth may or may not be willing to do so, the landlord settled on a compromise. Tiny and Ruth ended up losing their $250 deposit, which was more than they hoped for.

Tiny's travel authorization provided for him to drive to the coast, while Ruth and Dave would fly. With two cars to move, that created a minor problem. Jack White, having been away from California several months, agreed to take a few days off to drive one of the cars, and fly back to Columbus later. This would allow Ruth and Dave to visit Port Huron, and fly home after Tiny arrived. However, Dave would have no part of that delay. He chose to ride with Tiny, leaving his mom to make the trip alone! With Dave and Tiny in one car, and Jack in the other, they set out for California May 17 planning to drive straight through.

The night before Tiny, Dave, and Jack departed, three tornadoes touched down in the Columbus area, which certainly urged them on their way! The trip was made with but one incident. Planning to travel Interstate 40 out of Saint Louis, for some reason Jack turned toward Kansas City. By the time Tiny doubled back to catch him, he was nowhere in sight! Tiny was resigned to the fact that they would not see each other again until their arrival in Garden Grove. Noticing that his gas tank was nearing the empty mark, Tiny began looking for a station. The first one he spotted was closed. A few miles later, seeing one that appeared to be open, Tiny turned off only to find Jack at the station with a flat tire! What a miracle! Thereafter Tiny and Jack were very careful to stay within shouting distance.

After reaching California, they rented a motel in the Belmont Shores area of Long Beach where they stayed for about 6 weeks. Then Tiny found a house for sale in Garden Grove that they liked. While still at the motel, Tiny and Dave checked out the Little League situation. Since the season was by then half over, they figured there would be no openings for Dave, but things worked out very nicely. The manager of the Minor "A" White Sox was giving up his team for personal reasons. Harvey Langham, the manager of the Orioles, arranged for Tiny to take over the White Sox with Dave on his roster. The head to head competition with old Harv made life more interesting; however, Tiny found motel living, baseball practices, and playing scheduled games are not the best combination. In June 1973 Tiny and Ruth closed escrow on their house. Back on Acacia, the family was only 15 blocks from the place they left to go to Ohio. Dave was back in the same school, which was very much to his delight.

Cal Groves had Tiny lined up to be Inspection Supervisor, replacing another old friend, Russ Dickens, who was retiring his stamp. Though Tiny was not real anxious to be a supervisor again, he would have accepted anything just to be back in earthquake country! Tiny's manager was Jim Dick, another old friend, and Tiny's good buddy, John Harris, was also a supervisor in the group. Unlike the 1st day at Columbus, Tiny felt right at home. Cal knew all along Tiny had no desires to be back in management, and that he eventually wanted to go back to S&ID. Cal and Tiny had a verbal understanding that Tiny would remain on the Sabreliner program for no more than 1 year, after which Tiny would be free to seek a transfer to Downey. By then, Tiny had been away from Inspection long enough to have forgotten the hassles that go with the job.

Before long, Tiny was back into the swing of things. Writing repairs for discrepant hardware, assuring the equalization of overtime, and answering union grievances kept him busy. He and his family quickly renewed old friendships, and had no trouble resuming former patterns with friends and relatives. Tiny's brother Cliff and his family, and Ruth's brother Harry (Bud) and his family, all lived nearby. However, they could not be sure how long Bud would be nearby. Bud had developed a habit of buying a house, remodeling to suit his fancy, and then moving to another place that was a challenge to his "fixing up" skills. Moves became frequent enough that his wife Jeri only unpacked the necessities after each move.

Among others, Tiny and Ruth renewed their friendship with John Harris, Bob and Marylyn Claytor, the Callaways, and Tiny's cousin Delores (Dee) Mitchell and her husband Don. They played a lot of Pinochle with Dee and Don until they moved to Foresthill, near Sacramento. Of course, the Langhams were contacted immediately upon Tiny and his family's return to California. Don and Lynn Shearer had moved to Minnesota, where both were teaching school.

In the lapse of only a few years, Orange County had really grown in population, and new homes were springing up all over. The Santa Ana Freeway now extended to San Diego and beyond (to the border of Mexico), while I-405 (the San Diego Freeway) been completed to intersect with the Santa Ana near El Toro Marine Base. Traffic northbound in the morning and southbound in the afternoon had quickly outgrown the freeways, making Tiny's 50-mile trip commute to work tedious at best. But, Tiny wasn't complaining! He'd take freeway traffic and earthquakes over thunderstorms, tornadoes, and snow any day!

In May, 1974, a little short of the 1 year he had agreed to spend on the Saberliner, Tiny was offered his old job title at Seal Beach. With no personnel responsibility, the position was what Tiny had been looking for and his commuting time would be cut by 80%! With Cal's blessing, Tiny accepted the transfer to the Seal Beach Quality Assurance audit group and reported to his new boss—a woman! Tiny had no problem with this, but he sensed that because of his earlier supervisory experience, she saw him as a threat. He very quickly assured her that he had no desire for a management position, and that seemed to satisfy her concerns. Tiny and his new boss worked well together thereafter.

The 1974 Little League season began in April, with Dave and Tiny active from the beginning. Dave joined the senior division (13-15 years old). The teams played on a regulation size diamond and, for the first time, would be allowed to "lead off". The pitching distance of 60 feet, 6 inches was 14 feet, 6 inches farther than for Little League Majors, but Dave was a strong lad. Achieving the extra distance required would be no problem for him. Tiny and Dave's team (the Orioles) did not do well in '74. The team lacked experience finishing in last place. Dave was unable to finish the season because he broke an arm trying to break up a double play. Having seen the Pros execute a rolling block to take out a pivot man, he decided to try and ended up rolling on his own arm. Such is the price of experience!

The one thing they did accomplish during the season was overall improvement in the play of the younger team members. This would be a definite asset in the coming year because these players would be returning, which should give them a nucleus for the development of a better ball club.

About 3 a.m., July 4, 1974 Bill Engles called to advise Tiny and Ruth that his beloved wife, Shirley, had passed away about an hour earlier. One of her last requests, he said, was for him to call Ruth immediately. Her death was quite a blow to everyone, as she was only 35 years old at the time. Her loss hit Ruth extremely hard, as Shirley's passing was almost like losing a daughter.

With Tiny back at Seal Beach, the 10-mile round trip between Garden Grove and the plant was a big relief from the hassles of the San Diego Freeway, and that 50 mile grind. Unfortunately, the position at Seal Beach would last only about 6 months. Budget cuts were again taking their toll. By November, the audit function became the latest casualty. The entire group was placed on "open transfer", an impersonal situation in which job placement is subject to availability and requisitions for the affected classification. The alternative was layoff. After 26 years with the company, being laid off was the last thing Tiny wanted or expected. Fortunately, those employees in the audit group were well known to management in Downey, and were transferred there, including Tiny. He rejoined Emmett Edwards in Configuration Management. Test site support was the only Apollo activity remaining in Downey, and this effort was being phased out at a rapid pace. Although Rockwell had been chosen as the prime contractor for the Space Shuttle, recall of laid off employees and new hiring had not yet begun. The only Space Shuttle activity was centered on the preparation of procedures that would be used by the various support groups. Emmett had been assigned the responsibility to head up this activity. Tiny was appointed Emmett's group leader.

On January 19, 1975 Tiny and Ruth's daughter, Carole, gave birth to her fifth child, Michael, bringing the grandchildren count to seven. Shortly after the birth of Michael, Tiny discovered he had diabetes. Other than normal childhood diseases, he had never been sick. The doctor didn't require Tiny to take insulin; but, he put him on a strict diet of 1200 calories a day. In a little more than 3 months, Tiny dropped 25 pounds, and his blood sugar was under control.

In October, 1975 Tiny's mother agreed to leave Ashland and come to California to live. Cliff and Tiny flew home (this was the last time Tiny would go through that torture) and Bootie, whom the other family members had not seen in almost 30 years, came in from Baltimore. What a great reunion! They relived their boyhood days in Ashland and got caught up on happenings of the past 30 years. With some difficulty, the three brothers readied their mother for the trip west. Her natural reluctance to leave the area and her friends after so many years was compounded by news that her sister, Ethyl, had passed away. The brothers feared the bad news would give her cause to cancel the move, which probably would have happened if not for Cliff's counseling and persuasion. Very quickly they disposed of their mother's furniture, closed her bank account, and tied up other loose ends. After their mother's tearful goodbyes to relatives and her various friends, Cliff, Tiny, and their mother boarded a plane for California with Bootie returning to his family in Baltimore. Tiny's mother's move was to last no more than 8 months before she bought a bus ticket back to Ashland. In addition to missing old friends and relatives, the California style living just did not suit her tastes.

In 1976, one of Dave's friends gave him a pup of about 6 weeks, a mix of German Sheppard and Collie. Lacking a name, the family tagged him "Puppy". The name stuck. Sometime later the family added a cat "Chester", only to learn that Chester was a misnomer. He was a she! All of which establishes that in naming pets, the Gillum family took no awards.

On May 13, Pearl Spence called to let the Gillum's know that Buster had passed away. His mitral valve problems had been haunting him once more. He had gone into the hospital for what, by then, had become routine surgery. As before, Buster survived the surgery, but succumbed to undetected internal bleeding. This caused Tiny untold grief, because Buster had felt more like a brother to him than a friend.

The 1976 Little League was Dave's last in the senior division, and Tiny's final year of coaching him. During Dave's senior division career, he pitched one no-hitter and a couple of one-hitters, and was selected to the league's All-Star team in 1975 and 1976. His next step would be the Big League division, which accommodated 16-18 year olds. Although Tiny no longer coached Dave, he continued to coach in Little League for several more years.

In the drafts of 1977, Tiny chose a 13-year-old named Jeff Edwards. Though unknown at the time, Tiny also drafted two good friends, his mother, Pat, and his father, Tom. Later, Tom and Tiny coached together on several teams, including the senior division, two Big League championship squads, as well as at the high school level. Jeff's brothers, Ken and Chris, played on several of their teams.

Meanwhile, on the work front, in addition to his group leader duties, Tiny frequently was assigned special projects, particularly where trouble-shooting was involved. In the spring of 1977, Arrowhead Products in Los Alamitos (approximately 4 miles from Tiny's driveway) was awarded a contract by Rockwell to manufacture liquid oxygen and liquid hydrogen feed lines for the space shuttle. A special team from Rockwell (including members of the Engineering, Manufacturing, Procurement, and Quality Assurance organizations) was formed to monitor progress at the supplier's facility. The team was assigned on a temporary basis, but full time, and was responsible for assuring that disciplines were in place to meet contractual requirements, as well as established delivery schedules. A call from the team leader to Tiny's boss expressed concern about the supplier's compliance with Configuration Management, as well as Quality requirements. An audit of the supplier was requested, which ended up being Tiny's responsibility.

Following standard audit procedures, Tiny immediately realized the system at Arrowhead Products lacked discipline, and, in fact, was out of control! An adequate method for records retention did not exist. They had not so much as a clue about ADP preparation. This "go take a look" order from Tiny's boss ended up being an 8-month assignment, which was fine with him. Being only 10 minutes from work sure beat the drive on the freeway to and from Downey each day!

To begin resolving the problems at Arrowhead Products, Tiny recruited his friend and longtime co-worker, Bob Sherohman to assist. With Bob's assistance, Tiny was ready to go to work. The two men established a Records Control center, where all records were kept under lock and key. They also assumed responsibility for ADP preparation. Additionally, their duties included data reviews with the NASA personnel to gain their approval of the accumulated data prior to delivery of each feed line. Relieving them of a heavy burden, Arrowhead, of course, posed no objection to this arrangement.

During the long hours spent in that data accumulation room Tiny met Bud Buford, a Rockwell procurement resident manager, and probably the most hard-nosed man Tiny ever knew regarding establishing and meeting schedules. Bud and Tiny would see a lot of each other in the months and years to come!

Following the stint at Arrowhead Products, and back to his normal duties, things were becoming very hectic. Delivery of the first space shuttle, designated Orbiter 101, was drawing near. By that time, the shuttle was in Palmdale for final checkout prior to delivery to the Kennedy Space Center. Due to a lack of experienced personnel in Palmdale, crews from Downey were assigned the task of periodically aiding the cause at that facility. Although the trips were for only 1 week at a time, they were not welcomed by most of the men.

Over the years during their marriage, Ruth and Tiny made several trips to Port Huron. Tiny found her family to be a group of very fine people and quite competitive in sports, as well as card playing sessions, which, of course, Tiny liked. Moreover, Tiny always felt a wager, even small, made things more interesting! Ruth, unlike her father, sister, and brother, did not share the spirit of the wager. To her, a game was simply a game; win, lose, or draw, but get involved in competition with any of the rest, and one had better be ready for action! The card game of Euchre is a classic example.

As with most families, one member always stands out. Norval (Norv) Schattler was such a person in Ruth's family. Slow moving, slow talking, and a Lee Marvin look alike, Norv marched to the beat of a different drummer. He moved with the flow and never created waves. Tiny suspected if there was no more than family, boats, planes, and trains, Norv would have been perfectly satisfied to sit for hours watching any, or all of them. Tiny was sure Norv had seen every nature program ever aired on TV.

Norv and Tiny shared some commonalities. Neither liked broccoli but both liked McDonald's hamburgers. Neither could tolerate those stupid TV commercials or had a problem with sitting all day! Both men also liked golf. On one of Norv's visits from Port Huron, he and Tiny played a local course. On one hole, a par-4, he was on the green in two, and sank a long putt for a birdie! Tiny bought one of those "make your own" newspaper headlines proclaiming "Birdie Schattler invades Orange County", effectively nicknaming him "Birdie".

Don Shearer's beloved wife, Lynne, died of cancer March 3, 1977 at the age of 43. Her death was a major blow to Don because, in addition, to his love for life, he was quite dependent on her. Being severely crippled by arthritis, he was confined to a wheelchair. Through his grieving and handicap, Don never lost faith in God, facing his ordeal with dignity and poise. Just 2 short years later, on January 5, 1979, Don passed away, such a sad ending for such a competitive spirit. He and Tiny had shared their own version of the Olympics, called the "Sheargilathone"; horseshoes, ping pong, and shooting hoops. Only 54 at the time of his death, the rheumatoid arthritis had reduced Don from a robust, laughing character to little more than a shadow of himself.

In 1978, Tiny's friend, Bud Buford, called from the Marquardt Company in Van Nuys, California. Under contract to Rockwell, Marquardt was building the Primary and Vernier thruster engines used to maneuver the shuttle in space. They were, Bud said, experiencing some of the same problems encountered earlier at Arrowhead. He asked if Tiny could assist him. The assignment was not as long as that of the Arrowhead task, Tiny was pleased to say, because for that short time he had a round trip commute of more than 100 miles each day. Tiny's job this time, rather than taking hold and doing, was simply a "show and tell" project.

On Tiny's 55th birthday, July 28, 1980, he became eligible for retirement. He had no immediate plans, but knew the time had come for him to start making preparations for that long sought day. By that time Tiny had moved from the Shuttle primary program to a new support program called Payload Integration, again working for Emmett. Their task was to accumulate data in support of the various payloads the shuttle would carry into space and launch into orbit. The hardware would be manufactured under a new low cost concept similar to the Lockheed "skunk works". This concept, designed to preserve quality and safety, minimized paperwork as a cost savings measure. Once implemented, this system proved to be very successful in meeting both schedule and cost goals!

In October of 1981, Cath and Norv said goodbye to the cold weather of Port Huron and settled in San Luis Obispo, California. This left only Ruth's dad, her brother Bob, and his family in the land of the Wolverine. The move brought the sisters to within 230 miles of each other, as opposed to 2000 miles before. That pleased Ruth and Cath very much! Norv, too, as he no longer had to shovel snow!

Tiny continued to coach baseball in the West Garden Grove Little League Senior Division through the 1981 season, followed by two seasons with the Big League team.

A Prelude to Retirement

They had no superstars in the 1982 and 1983 seasons; but, they did have a bunch of boys who wanted to win ball games. A record of 35 wins and 4 losses earned their team the district title both years, making those years the most satisfying ones of Tiny's coaching career. Winning a game is always more satisfying than losing; but, the real gratification of those years was to be associated with such a nice bunch of boys. They made those years satisfying for Tiny. In addition the fine coaching support from Tom Edwards also contributed to the success of those teams. Jeanne Cash, as "team mother", handled all the financial duties, and the mountain of paperwork required by the league. She also kept the players supplied with licorice sticks (Tiny thought they looked more forward to the licorice than the playing of games). Pat Edwards took care of the score keeping duties; Tiny's wife, Ruth, kept everyone supplied with all her delicious cookies, which she was famous for; and, George Cash was the number 1 cheerleader!

March 3, 1982 Tiny's mother passed away from what was determined to be natural causes. Her death was followed by the death of Ruth's father November 2 from heart failure. Tiny's fear of flying prevented him from attending either funeral. He had long before reached an understanding with his mother on that. She knew that, when the time came, her son Tiny would be there if he could do so any other way than flying. Cliff and Tiny started to drive home for the funeral, but developed car trouble in Arizona. By the time repairs were made, they did not have sufficient time to continue and arrive for the funeral in time. They returned home, and Cliff and his daughter Mimi flew back for the funeral.

Tiny continued to work in Payload Integration through 1983. In October that year, he concluded he would "hang it up", which he did January 27, 1984, bringing this dozen years to a close. Tiny and Ruth moved toward another chapter in their lives, anticipating happy days of retirement.

***

CHAPTER 9

The Retirement Years

January 1, 1984 was more than just a day to watch football games for Tiny. This day was the beginning of the final countdown to retirement. He was really excited! Just 27 days later Tiny would be saying a final goodbye to the place where he had spent most of his adult life. Tiny was sure there must have been mixed emotions. However, he only recalled the anticipation.

Assignments at work kept Tiny busy making the days pass quickly. Suddenly, the "day" arrived! After 35 years, 5 months, and 17 days, Tiny turned in his picture badge ending a career at the same Rockwell facility where his career began, Downey. Then was the time to "ride off into the sunset". Instead, Tiny turned south toward home (had he gone west, his hat would have been floating in about 1 hour!).

A few days before that final day, co-workers threw a retirement party for Tiny, showering him with gifts and advice on how to spend his retirement years. He and Ruth, of course, had discussed what to do after retirement many times, but without making any firm plans. Likes, dislikes, dreams, and concerns about retirement would have to be sorted out. They planned to take their time doing that.

That first Monday after retirement began was a strange sensation for Tiny. The "early to rise" habits, formed over so many years, refused to go away. He found himself wide awake by 6 a.m. Waking up early without having to may seem foolish to those yet to experience that situation;

but, old habits, like old dogs, cannot be taught new tricks. At least, that was the case with Tiny!

One of Tiny and Ruth's first indulgences was a new car. Their old one, with the equivalent of three trips around the world on the odometer, also deserved retirement. If, as they planned, they were to travel, a new car was hardly an extravagance; buying a new car was a necessity. After much shopping, they settled for a Nissan Maxima, which proved to be a good choice. With Tiny having taken a 1-year sabbatical leave from coaching, he and Ruth then had the freedom, the time, and the means to travel. Those who told Tiny how difficult "adjusting" to retirement would be were in for a surprise. Tiny found the transition very easy. He missed seeing friends at work, of course, but then he had a boss he could deal with…HIMSELF! If he got out of line, he could "tell him off" while shaving, and never fear being fired! As circumstances turned out, he's been pretty easy to work for, and other than an occasional reminder that he can't penalize himself, Tiny and his boss during retirement had very little trouble getting along with each other. *In all honesty*, Tiny thought, *retirement has been the best job I have ever had!*

Other than a trip to the Sacramento area looking for a suitable retirement site, Tiny and Ruth stayed pretty close to home in 1984. They did spend a few days with Cath and Norv, and took a couple of excursions to Las Vegas though. They found nothing to their liking around Sacramento, but did like the Santa Maria area quite well. In fact, they placed a deposit on a very nice mobile home there. However, in time after prolonged consideration, they discarded the idea of moving there; although, they forfeited their small deposit, they thought not moving there was the proper decision. Prior to the time Tiny faced the option, he may have been inclined to wonder why his elders were so reluctant to resettle, his mother being a case in point. Faced with similar decisions, Tiny and Ruth discovered that roots planted deeply are not easily uprooted. There were friends, first and foremost, that they simply did not want to abandon. They also considered having to change doctors and medical facilities they knew for the unknown. Aside from that, in their case, there were

Ruth's interests in her craft classes, and Tiny's baseball interests in the area.

Being a country music fan, Tiny was sobered by the death of his favorite singer of all time, Ernest Tubb September 6, 1984. Having admired him as, in Tiny's opinion, "the greatest" singer of the "only" music, country, caused Tiny to reflect. He remembered listening to Ernest Tubb on radio and honky-tonk juke boxes when he was 16, or so. Tubb's rendition of "I'm Walking' the Floor over You" would always be Tiny's favorite country song. One of Tiny's most memorable gifts came from Ruth, who treated him to one of Ernest Tubb's few Southern California appearances shortly before his death.

By the end of his 1st year of retirement, Tiny had grown to love the easy life. He was busy doing nothing. He wondered how he ever managed time for work. Tiny received several "offers" during that 1st year; some with very good salaries, but he liked the no deadline, no obligation life too much. Thus, he turned all the job offers down. Not so, however, with coaching baseball. That being a labor of love could never be denied.

After the 1985 baseball season ended and Ruth's craft class ended at about the same time that seemed to be an excellent time to hit the road. First stop, Port Huron, Michigan followed by visits to Ashland, Nashville, Baltimore, and a 1-week stopover in Reno, Nevada on the way home. Gone a total of 7 weeks, they concluded that was too long to be away and especially too long to spend in any "open gambling" city.

Tiny and Ruth enjoyed 3 days in Nashville at the Opryland Hotel. While there they took in some outstanding country music shows. Another highlight of the Nashville trip was a side trip to Lynchburg, Tennessee where they toured the Jack Daniels Distillery. For Tiny, this was a very fascinating experience well worth the few extra miles driven and time spent to see such a fabulous attraction.

Tiny and Ruth's friendship with Harv and Virginia Langham prospered over the years coming to look upon them as "family". They had two children, Ron and Carrie.

Harv was a much laid back unpretentious individual. His attitude, sometimes puzzling to Tiny, left no doubt that Harv would never have to deal with anxiety. Virginia, on the other hand, was a worrier. She worried over having nothing to worry about.

Virginia also was always ready to help, whether friend, family, or stray cat. Additionally, she was a hard worker at home and on the job at Houser Company, where she was the office manager serving as Cliff Houser's right arm. Another trait of Virginia's was a penchant for expression, in her own way, using her own version of the English language. Tiny thought, *her amazing ability to speak in what is a very unique manner has never ceased to amaze me.* After a while he began to take notes of some of Virginia's most precious gems. As somewhat of a dabbler in rhyme, Tiny decided to write a poem that described this lady and her language. He entitled the poem "Virginiaese":

Virginiaese

We have this friend, who talks very strange,
    She will make you slap both your knees.
Sit back, relax, and I will arrange,
    A lesson in Virginiaese.

We were driving the freeway one Saturday night,
    Our exit was just up ahead.
I cut down my speed, and signaled a right,
    It was then that this lady said.

"Why is he letting those other cars by?
    Please tell me, I really must know.
Did we have a flat, or run out of gas,
    Why is he speeding so slow?"

As we ordered lunch in a Palm Springs café,
    The waitress was shocked there's no doubt
We wanted two checks for convenience of pay,
    But this is the way it came out.

"Harvey don't add with the greatest of ease,
    And Gill ain't really too swift.
Could we have two separate menus please?
    It might just prevent a big rift!"

When Harvey returned the tile he had bought,
    (He was reckless, and broke quite a few).
She quickly provided the answer I sought,
    When I asked her how well did he do?

"I didn't go with him, I just didn't dare,
    But it must have been well worth his while.
I really don't know what transcribed over there,
    But he sure came home with new tile!"

We converted our money for a vacation trip,
    Each traveler's check was a twenty.
To tell our dear friend was a definite slip,
    Her action was predictably plenty.

"Some should be larger to me it would seem,
    You are much more practical I thought.
I just can't believe in my wildest dreams,
    That's the only dimension you bought.

Now Casey Stengel sure knew double talk,
    And Yogi Berra could clown.
If they met head to head it would be a cakewalk
    This lady would talk them both down!

Written by D. V. Gillum

Others not set to rhyme, but favorites of Tiny's were:

> **Virginiaese**: "I saw a house on a big empty lot today that I liked very much."
> **Translation**: I saw a house today sitting alone on a big lot that I liked very much.
> **Virginiaese**: "The traffic on Beach Boulevard was due to a backed up accident.
> **Translation**: The traffic on Beach Boulevard was backed up due to an accident.

Back on the baseball front, at the beginning of 1985, Tiny had decided he would coach in the Little League Senior Minor division, where he could work strictly with 13 year olds who were experiencing their 1st year of play on a regulation field. These young players needed to learn many things. In 1986, the "Red Sox" rewarded Tiny with an excellent season by winning the league championship and the Garden Grove city championship, as well. The most enjoyable part of winning the championship game for Tiny was the manner in which the team came from behind to do so, and that was with having a part-time player provide the heroics. Not only did he knock in the winning run, he was also the winning pitcher in relief of the team's starting pitcher! Just for Tiny to see the joy on that player's face made all the long hard hours spent with these boys well worth the effort. Tom Edwards and Tiny were elected coaches for the 13-year-old All-Star team that year. That year Tiny's team came within one win of going to Sacramento for the state tournament.

Starting his 4th year of retirement as 1987 approached, Tiny discovered that time really does fly when you are having fun! That year brought a significant change in his coaching activities. The varsity coach at Pacifica High School asked Tiny to coach their freshman team. Although flattered by the invitation, Tiny had reservations. First, he was not sure he'd be comfortable coaching at the high school level; not only because doing so would be a salaried position, but because he felt the pressure to win would be much greater than in Little League. He had always maintained that when coaching became a "job", he would step down.

Coaching in Little League is a voluntary task. Winning is important, but not a primary goal (at least for Tiny it wasn't). Parents want a winner, and so do the children, but although Tiny liked to win, there were more important considerations for him.

If Tiny accepted the coaching position at the high school, he felt that he would be expected to win at all costs. That was not the case. The varsity coach assured Tiny that his assumptions were wrong, that pressure to win was not a part of his program, and that the freshman team would be his to coach on a non-interference basis. All the high school coach asked was that Tiny coach his own way with a view to preparing the players for the varsity. After much consideration, Tiny accepted the offer.

In February, 1987 Tiny began his high school coaching career. He had a big advantage over other members of the coaching staff, having coached most of the kids in Little League, he was aware of their talents and abilities. Since most of the players had been through Tiny's routine before, practices were easier for everyone.

Coaching high school players was no bed of roses for Tiny. Undesirable features were daily practices (hardly a retirement routine), field preparation, and bus rides to and from games played on the road. Even so, Tiny treasured the experience. After one season at the freshman level, he was moved up to the position of junior varsity coach. Tiny continued coaching through the 1990 season, completing 4 very successful years at the high school level. During those years, the junior varsity players compiled an overall record of 62 wins and 23 losses. Tiny sent some very talented athletes to the varsity team.

In June, 1988, Ruth's brother Bob moved to California following the breakup of his marriage. The last of the Emerson clan to leave Port Huron for the balmy climate of

The Retirement Years

California, Bob lived with Tiny and Ruth for about 10 months. One of those people who had to keep busy, Bob was a big help to Tiny. Not only did Bob help Tiny paint the house, but he relieved him of the need to accompany Ruth on weekly marketing chores, a task Tiny despised. Following a short stay with Cath and Norv in San Luis Obispo, Bob ended up settling in the Sacramento area.

The year 1988, though not a bad one in personal terms, was a time of sadness. In October, Tiny's best friend, George Belcher, suffered a stroke that would take its toll on him in later years. He spent time in the hospital but later returned to work. George was one that thrived on daily work activity and contact with co-workers. Subsequent to the initial stroke, he suffered two more, and, sadly, May 9, 1992 (during the time of Tiny's writing his autobiography) Tiny's friend George passed away at his home in Fountain Valley, California. Goodie, his devoted wife and companion stood by him to the end. She insisted that when the medics could do no more for him, he be brought home to spend his final hours in familiar surroundings, among those who loved, admired, and respected him. Tiny, along with others, missed George, having no one else to ever take his place.

On November 11, 1988, Tiny's Aunt Earl died. She was the one, along with her late husband Harry, who did so many things for Tiny when he was a child to lighten, what would, otherwise, have been a much heavier load. Tiny had not seen his aunt for several years, but nothing diminished the memories. He was saddened not to have seen her more often. It is, Tiny thought, a sad commentary on the society in which we live that imbues us with so much assurance of an everlasting future…there's never enough time, yet we always think there will be time, some other time. If, in writing this, Tiny achieved no more than to remind its readers (then or in the future) how fleeting life can be, and to admonish others not to forget that fact, he felt he will have made a contribution.

Tiny's old faithful dog, Puppy, turned 13 in December, 1988. That was equivalent to about 91 years in human terms. He had, by then, developed arthritis in both hind legs, making walking progressively more difficult. The pain Puppy suffered could not be diminished by drugs so on April 17, 1999 Tiny carried him, with misgivings akin to mortal sin, to the animal hospital to be put to sleep. Nothing short of transplants of both hips, he was told, would give Puppy relief. He also had a tumor on one side that was inoperable. The dog was in a no-win situation. Tiny's only solace was in the knowledge that he would no longer have to suffer. Putting down Puppy, the family pet was not an easy decision for Tiny. For years afterwards, Tiny felt the pain of losing Puppy. After Puppy's passing, Tiny and his family resolved to "never" own another dog, for no other could take Puppy's place in their heart.

In the spring of 1990, another lady came into Tiny's life. She was not yet a year old. This lovely child, Amanda, was the daughter of a single parent Laura, to whom Tiny and Ruth had been introduced by their son, Dave. This lovely little lady with her blue eyes, blonde hair, and happy disposition, wasted no time in capturing Tiny and Ruth! She and her mother spent considerable time at the Gillum home, and soon were considered part of the family.

At the end of the 1990 baseball season, Tiny put away his baseball coaching shoes with far more reservations than when he turned in his badge at Rockwell. This ended 18 years of working with great children in a sport he loved as dearly as life itself. Tiny wasn't sure he'd be able to handle that loss; and, at times, felt like giving up coaching was a death sentence. Coaching had become such an important part of Tiny's life that he needed something as a replacement. The only answer was golf. That, plus yard work so long neglected, kept Tiny busy, but simply could not fill the void. To express his feelings about the game he loved so much and enjoyed so fully, Tiny wrote the following:

Desires of a Coach

When I die, it matters not,
    Cremate me, or let me rot,
Bury me beneath the sea,
    Or, dig a regular grave for me.

I do not want to know, you see,
    The disposal method used for me,
But, I'm no different from the rest,
    There are some things that I request.

Before they close that coffin lid,
    To remind folks of the things I did,
And accentuate my life's demand,
    Place a baseball in my hand.

To go with me on my last ride,
    Put my glove in by my side,
Add my hat and my old spikes,
    A counter showing balls and strikes.

My stirrup socks down by my feet,
    The signs I used would be real neat,
Then rounding out this little scheme,
    A picture of my final team.

We can't appeal, there is no doubt,
    When the Master Umpire calls us out,
I can only take this one approach,
    I hope God needs a baseball coach!

Written by D. V. Gillum

With Tiny's coaching career over, he and Ruth turned their attention to the vacation they had planned for mid-July. They would visit Ruth's cousin Marion, and husband Jim Utt, in Decatur, Illinois, plus Tiny's Aunt Phoebe and Uncle Audie in Ashland. During the final stages of preparation for vacation, Tiny received a call from the inimitable "world famous" Bud Buford, saying he was in dire need of assistance once more. Rockwell had initiated a program called "Flex Force", employing retirees and others interested in full or part-time work to supplement their income. The program had already been approved by the IRS, and would not affect pensions. Bud wanted Tiny to come in for 8 to 10 weeks to help with problems he was experiencing at Marquardt once more. When Tiny told Bud they were leaving on vacation, Bud asked Tiny to think the offer over, and contact him on his return. Then they ended the conversation.

Departing Garden Grove July 15, Tiny and Ruth met Cliff and Norma in Barstow. There, they formed a two-car caravan. From Barstow they drove to Williams, Arizona, where they spent the night. The next morning the caravan drove to the Grand Canyon, where Tiny was in for a big surprise! He had never been there before, and from the pictures he had seen, had no real desire to see the site thinking the canyon was just another *big hole in the ground.* Well, as you must know, Tiny was wrong again! To Tiny, the Grand Canyon was the most awesome sight; one that defied description. Tiny recommended if you haven't been there, go at the first opportunity.

From the Grand Canyon, Tiny, Cliff, and their wives continued east to Branson, Missouri, the place that was giving Nashville a run for its money as the Country Music Capitol of the United States. Many of the big name stars had built theatres and night clubs there, and more were in the construction or planning stage. The town was either "famous" or "infamous" for the absolute worst traffic congestion Tiny had ever experienced. To Tiny, the traffic in Branson made California's freeway parking lots look like vacant prairies! Once a tourist entered Highway 76, he was trapped. Three lanes, with the center lane reserved for emergency vehicles. No passing was allowed. Once on that road, there was no turning back, or turning off except into theatre parking lots. They moved, if one can call it that, with the pace of the traffic, which was not very fast. They need not moan or groan, as there was no other alternative!

With prepaid reservations at the Hillbilly Motel, the foursome was obliged to stay longer than they might have, otherwise. They "braved" the highway a couple of times to see Boxcar Willie at his theatre, and to let the ladies do some shopping. Cliff and Tiny went golfing once, and that was one time too many! The course was apparently built by laying a 1 inch cover of sod over a rock quarry. You couldn't take a divot without making the rocks fly! The course, unlike the highway, was not crowded, and they had no problem figuring out why!

After Branson, the two couples spent a night in Mountain Home, Arkansas. The trip through the Ozark Mountains was beautiful. They also saw some very lovely homes. Compared to California, real estate prices there were a "steal". They toured some homes, much larger than most in California, with far more land, and in some cases, a boat dock. Those homes were priced for about half of what they would bring on the California real estate market. Tiny thought, *if I could take Orange County's climate with me, I might be tempted to live in the Ozarks.*

After a pleasant stay in Mountain Home, Tiny, his brother Cliff, and their wives set out for Ashland to visit Aunt Phoebe and Uncle Audie. Traveling through western Kentucky was quite scenic, and made Tiny wonder at the difference between there and the other end of the state, where he grew up. They arrived in Ashland July 25, just 3 days before Tiny's 65th birthday, planning to stay until the 28th. Their plans changed abruptly when Norma spied a cockroach in their motel room, prompting a move to another motel, which was no better, for Tiny spotted one that night in the bathroom! Fearful they might end up with roaches in their luggage and bring them home with them, they abandoned ship fast! Cliff and Tiny also canceled plans to play golf there. They only took time to have a local sign shop prepare a sign reading "Birthplace of D. V. Gillum". Then they headed out of town toward Wayland, the place of Tiny's birth.

Upon reaching Wayland, Tiny's intentions were to stand beside the Wayland town limits sign and have Ruth snap his picture. The journey took them, via Route 23, through Catlettsburg, Louisa, Paintsville, and Prestonsburg. At that point they turned off on Route 80, which is a scenic and very pleasant drive, although very narrow with many twists and turns. Route 80 took them to the Wayland turnoff, which is a state route but fortunately, a paved road. Soon they were at the Wayland town limits (population 600). There Tiny posed for Ruth to snap pictures, completing a cycle that begun 65 years before...almost to the day!

Wayland, with one street, and a few houses on each side resembling military barracks, took only a few minutes to see. What stood out the most about Wayland to Tiny was how the town limits signs were peppered with bullet holes! That reminded him of the summer in 1930, when they were on their way to Uncle Ed's place. Tiny recalled his father repeatedly demonstrating his skills shooting his pistol at partially driven nails in trees—usually hitting them dead center!

The Retirement Years

After Wayland, next stop was Lexington, Kentucky. Adjacent to their motel was a restaurant called the "Cracker Barrel", one of a popular chain of restaurants in the south. Specializing in "home cooking", they also sold jellies, jams, and country smoked hams. Cliff and Norma were so impressed with the blackberry jelly, they wanted to buy some to take home...until they discovered the labels proclaimed the jelly to have been prepared and packaged in California! So much for the use of "local talent" in the preparation of that good old "Southern home cooking", which Tiny and Cliff once knew and enjoyed.

From Lexington, the caravan drove to Lima, Ohio for a short visit with Jayhanny, whom they had not seen for several years. Tiny and Ruth stayed only 1 night because they had promised Jim and Marion we would be arriving at their place before the end of the month. Thus, the caravan formed at Barstow broke up in Lima. From Lima, Cliff and Norma were heading for the Dayton, Ohio area to visit Norma's relatives. Ruth and Tiny would be stopping over in Las Vegas on the way home. Cliff and Norma were driving straight home from Dayton.

Tiny and Ruth's visit with Jim and Marion proved to be a highlight of the trip. They really went all out to make the Gillum's visit a joy. Tiny had hoped to get in a round of golf with Jim, but had to cancel that. Jim was having trouble with a leg that restricted his ability to move about. Instead, they had plenty of good (real) home cooked food, and lots of conversation.

Tiny and Ruth started home August 1 after a few days in Las Vegas, arriving home on Dave's 30th birthday, August 7. After 3 weeks on the road, and most of the nights in motels, being home in their own bed was nice! The following morning Tiny called Bud Buford as he had promised and learned that he was still interested in having Tiny come to Marquardt.

After about 6 weeks of negotiations regarding salary, Tiny became un-retired (if only temporary) September 28. After 7 years of retirement, Tiny questioned whether he could be of any help to Bud, or anyone for that matter. The answer was not long in coming. Just as if he'd never been away, Tiny was back into his job almost from the 1st day.

Marquardt had experienced a large turnover in Quality Assurance personnel and somewhere along the way; systems installed in the 1970's were no longer being utilized fully. Data reviews, once routine, were consuming too much time, costing too much, and impacting established delivery schedules. All of this was due to lack of experienced employees at both Marquardt and Rockwell. The situation was a classic case of the blind leading the blind! Identifying the problems and implementing corrective actions was not that difficult. With the advantage of prior experience in such fields, they had things back in focus in a very short time; reviews were being conducted without delay and with no major problems.

At Marquardt Tiny had joined a team similar to the one at Arrowhead Products in the 1970's, with one significant difference. We were only a team of three, plus a source inspector already assigned to Marquardt. Aside from Bud, the team leader, the other team member was a long time Rockwell employee named Frank O'leary. Frank also was a flex force employee and was very well versed in the scheduling and planning functions. Although Frank had worked for Rockwell for several years, that was his and Tiny's first meeting. By the time of Christmas break, the three team members working together had the problems pretty well turned around.

In January, 1991, Bud, Frank, and Tiny returned to complete the task. By then most of the hardware had been delivered; but, there was still work to be done. The team's activity would then be focused on eliminating any bottlenecks that might create delivery constraints. These included problems in engineering change control, planning, and scheduling. They also did a lot of "bird dog" work in the manufacturing and testing areas to assure delivery of a quality product on time. By mid-February, the team's work was completed. Hardware was flowing, Bud and his boss were happy, and Tiny's flex force assignment was done. Once more Tiny could retire, and chew his boss out through the shaving mirror, or ignore him if he chose. With no more schedules to meet, Tiny returned to a life of leisure!

Before Tiny and Ruth were to take another vacation, they learned, much to their dismay, that Dave's friend Laura had accepted a job in Missouri, and would be leaving and, of course, taking their delightful little Amanda with her. They had become a big part of the Gillum's lives. Knowing they would not be there when Tiny and Ruth returned from their next trip made leaving "such sweet sorrow". Laura tried to talk Dave into going with them but, having left California once (against his own desires); he could not bring himself to do so again.

For some years, Ruth and Tiny had thought of visiting Pacific Northwest and British Columbia. June 16 they headed north on Highway 101, via San Francisco. The "coast route", unlike Interstate 5, is a scenic highway. They saw parts of California they had never and otherwise might never have seen. They were enthralled with the beauty and cleanliness of San Francisco and vowed to return at a later date to take in more of the city by the Golden Gate.

The trip took Tiny and Ruth through California's giant redwoods, spectacular to behold and pretty. However, Tiny found that leg of the journey a bit monotonous due to the abundance of the same thing mile after mile. In Oregon and Washington, they were met with those states' greatest claim to fame—rain! *Somewhere over that area*, Tiny thought, *they must have the garden hose of the world. If they could turn it off, I'm sure they would.* Oregon and Washington also had more than their fair share of traffic!

In Victoria, British Columbia, Tiny and Ruth also encountered rain, but not enough to prevent them from touring Butchart Gardens. After spending a night at the Waddling Dog Inn, they enjoyed a nice ferry boat ride back to the mainland. San Francisco, Victoria Island and a jet boat ride on the Rouge River were the memorable highlights of the trip. On their way home, they took a 1-day side trip to Lake Tahoe. However, they saw nothing on the entire trip that remotely compared to vacations spent in New England and the southern states. At that point, they concluded that in the event they decided to change retirement locale, they would not be moving to Oregon or Washington!

While on vacation, Tiny and Ruth had boarded their cat, Chester, at the animal hospital as usual. Chester always acted a bit strange when they picked her up after previous trips. Normally, she would be nervous and cry for a few days, but this time her behavior was different. Finally concluding she was really in pain, they took her back to the hospital for examination. Tests revealed she was suffering from kidney failure. With no assurance that treatment could resolve the problem, once more, they had to confront the decision of what would be better for the pet. Putting pets down is never easy but sometimes has to be done. With Chester's situation, putting her down was in her best interest. On July 29 she was mercifully put to sleep. The Gillum's had no more pets after Chester's passing.

September 3, 1991 Charlie O'Connor, Ruth's ex-husband and the father of Pete, Biff, and Carole, passed away. His death was saddening because Tiny and Ruth had remained friends with him and his mother, Tress, over the years since he and Ruth divorced. Tiny always enjoyed having chitchats with him because he was well versed on many topics and was a very interesting man. Charlie was a tinkerer. He could not, or would not, leave anything he owned in its original state. He took things apart and modified them to suit his own specifications. His bedroom was more of a workshop than a place to sleep. Along one side of the room he built a work bench that accommodated every hand tool and small power tool known to man. In his living room he had three or four television sets with an equal amount of VCRs, all operated by remote control. He also had a camcorder for taping programs that interested him, which were more than a few. This amazing man recorded his own Last Will and Testament, which he gave to Pete with instructions to view only after his death.

Tiny later assisted Pete in the removal of Charlie's personal belongings from his Long Beach apartment. In addition to a couple of trailer loads, clearing the apartment took 11 trips with a pickup truck to empty three rooms! But don't get the idea the apartment was messy; it was not. Tiny was amazed at how neatly and conveniently everything was arranged in his living quarters.

"Tugboat Tessie", as Charlie's mother, Tress, was known, hailed from the state of Michigan. Tiny explained why she was called "The Fabulous Tugboat Tessie". As a teenager, Tress helped her father deliver mail by boat on the Great Lakes; hence the nickname. September 17, 1991 she celebrated her 98th birthday, but looked and acted more like 68. In addition to being a Great Lakes sailor, she had been white water rafting on the Colorado River, had appeared with Wink Martindale on the television show "Tic-Tac-Dough" and had played a supporting role with Burt Lancaster in the film, Elmer Gantry.

After the loss of her husband, Biz, several years previously, Tress became self-sufficient. In 1992 at the time of Tiny's writing his autobiography *Recollections of a Common Man* Tress still had a valid California driver's license, worked as a volunteer 2 days a week at Saint Mary's Hospital in Long Beach, and still had time to "check in on friends" who were much younger than her 98 years. Both Tress and Charlie were considered part of the Gillum family. Tress was like a mother-in-law to both Ruth and Tiny. They always cherished her and treasured her friendship. When Tress was 90 years old, Tiny wrote the following poem about her:

Ode to Tugboat Tessie

With laughs and tears, through ninety years,
    This gal has seen a lot.
And through it all, she's had a ball,
    Gave lots of things a shot.

First job she had, was with her Dad,
    As his first mate, no less.
She gained much fame, earned the name,
    Of lovely "Tugboat Tess".

At Mueller brass, she was the class,
    Of the female working sector.
Pound for pound, the best around,
    A top-notch parts inspector.

An avid fan, was the Governor man,
    Of the land of the Wolverine.
The bow tie kid, sure flipped his lid,
    When he met this snazzy queen!

But North wind blows, Port Huron snows,
    Soon got to be old stuff.
This lady whiz, and husband Biz,
    Said, "We have had enough."

With tearful eyes, they said goodbyes,
    To those they loved the best.
Then took the course, advised by Horace,
    "Go west young man, go west."

The Retirement Years

They headed straight, for the Golden State,
    Real thrilled to say the least.
So eager too, to start anew,
    Where she left off back east.

A real live spark, she made her mark,
    With volunteer work and such.
Then showed the master, Burt Lancaster,
    Her natural acting touch.

Staunch Democrat, a Dodger brat,
    Sure likes those cruising ships.
In full accord, first one aboard,
    For the Vegas fun bus trips.

Her lack of fear, was very clear,
    Though some folks thought her daft,
When she packed her grip, and took a trip,
    On a white water river raft.

She stole the show, on Tic-Tac-Dough,
    So sleek, refined, so dressy,
That handsome male, Wink Martindale,
    Sure loved our Tugboat Tessie.

Now Tugboat Tess, or Grandma Tress,
    Whichever you desire.
This lady fair, with silver hair,
    Will really light your fire.

Written by D. V. Gillum

As mentioned previously, Tiny was a devoted Cincinnati Reds fan! In the 1990 World Series the Reds rewarded him by defeating the Oakland Athletics. Moreover, the Reds' 1991 season gave Tiny more thrills than he could remember since he began following the grand old game as a child. While rooting for the Reds, Tiny put just as much effort into "booing" the Dodgers (both Brooklyn and Los Angeles versions). For many years Tiny had prided himself as being the number 1 Dodger hater. Then, a friend of Tiny's bragged to him that he "danced and jumped with joy" when a retired Dodger died. At that point, Tiny relinquished his claim to the title; although, he no longer claimed to be number 1, he was definitely a close 2nd in the "hate the Dodgers" club!

With the opening of the 1991 season, Tiny anticipated seeing the Reds repeat the glories of 1990. Though that wasn't the outcome, Tiny never diminished his anxiety and support for the Reds. The thrills Tiny received in the 1991 season didn't come from what the Reds achieved but from the Dodgers didn't achieve. At the time of the All-Star break in July the Dodgers had a five game lead over Tiny's beloved Reds. The situation looked bleak. Tiny chafed at the thought of the Dodgers winning the pennant, much less the World Series. At that time, a young upstart Atlanta Braves team was in 3rd place, 9.5 games behind the league leading Dodgers. Following the All-Star break the Reds fell flat on their collective faces, but not so the Braves. This gutsy bunch of relative newcomers to the league's high rent district kept whittling away at the Dodgers' lead. With only three games remaining in the season, the Braves not only caught the "invincible" Dodgers, they surpassed them by one game winning the pennant. Well did Tiny remember the day! With eyeballs glued to the TV, rooting for the Braves to defeat the Houston Astros and wishing the Dodgers only the worst of luck in their series in San Francisco.

Tiny's worrying was not necessary, as the Braves won 2 of 3 from Houston and San Francisco did the same to the Dodgers! On Saturday, October 5, the Braves clinched the Western division crown, earning the right to meet the Eastern division winning Pittsburgh Pirates in the National

League playoffs. Although not quite the same as seeing Tiny's Reds in the playoffs, seeing the Dodgers eliminated did him a world of good. Atlanta, as the records books will confirm, went on to defeat the Pirates in the playoffs.

The sixth game of that series was one of the most exciting Tiny had watched. A baby faced youngster named Steve Avery pitched a 1 to 0 shutout against Pittsburgh forcing a seventh game to be played. Tiny could hardly contain himself and was a nervous wreck before October 17 arrived. On that evening, the Braves capped what Tiny called a perfect season. With three runs in the first inning, they went on to win that seventh and final game 4 to 0. By winning, the Braves earned a spot in the World Series where they would play the Minnesota Twins, the American League champs. With his Reds out of play, Tiny didn't have any remorse at rooting for the Braves.

One evening in August while watching the Braves on television, Tiny saw an advertisement for the "Braves Baseball Heaven" Fantasy Camp. The camp, sponsored by the Braves and conducted in West Palm Beach, Florida, was scheduled for early February, 1992. Tiny felt a little twinge. He had always wanted to attend one of these camps, but never felt comfortable parting with the money involved for such a frivolous adventure. But, as they say, we buy what we want, not what we need. After discussing the matter with Ruth and his doctor, Tiny decided to go for it, and called for the brochure.

Those who follow baseball, if only intermittently, may recall that the 1991 World Series opened in Minneapolis, Minnesota October 19. The Twins delivered a two-game defeat to the Braves, and sent them back to Atlanta reeling. As they had done all year, the Braves came back to win all three games at home, and went back to Minnesota with a lead of 3 games to 2. With that, Tiny's mind was made up. He knew he had to attend that fantasy camp, now that the National League champs…and perhaps the World Series champs…would be conducting the event. With two games to play back in the METRODOME, Tiny expected some very exciting baseball…but was not prepared for what turned out to be the most exciting exhibition of Tiny's lifetime. Tiny really believed if the series had been more than seven games, his old heart would not have lasted. Both teams played outstanding baseball, but as the Twins had done before, they prevailed winning the series 4 games to 3. Although losing the series, that young band of Atlanta Braves had nothing to be ashamed about. They certainly played their hearts out!

With the World Series over, Tiny turned his attention to his own forthcoming "baseball season", the fantasy camp. He completed the enrollment form, and mailed the form with the required deposit. Enrollment costs included round trip air fare, but Tiny would have no need for that. He had long resolved to never fly again! Ruth's cousin, Dan, and his wife, Beulah, lived in Daytona Beach, Florida. Tiny and Ruth planned to drive to Daytona Beach allowing Ruth to spend time with her cousin and his family while Tiny was in West Palm Beach. When Cath and Norv expressed the desire to make the trip to see Dan and Beulah, the Gillum's travel plans changed. They decided to put Ruth and Cath on a plane, and Norv and Tiny would drive. Their return trip plans were for Cath and Norv to fly home while Ruth and Tiny drove. This arrangement relieved Ruth of driving both ways, and allowed Norv to see some of the country he had not seen before. Moreover, Tiny wanted Ruth to join him for the last 3 days of his fantasy. By flying one way, she would have more visiting time and still be able to share some of Tiny's baseball thrills.

With Thanksgiving and Christmas standing between Tiny and the fantasy camp in February, he faced a challenge. Although he walked about 3 miles a day, he would have to work harder at getting in physical condition. He needed to lose about 10 pounds (during the best eating time of the year) and get his throwing arm and running legs in shape.

During that same period of time, Tiny and Ruth celebrated their 35th wedding anniversary (December 10). As they normally did, they enjoyed a nice dinner out, and congratulated themselves on another year filled with happiness. *This is*, Tiny thought, *a good time to insert something else that deserves to be said. I could never have found a more resilient, more cooperative, more supportive, or more loving woman than Ruth*…and he thanked God daily for bringing her into his life!

Tiny's feeling that Christmas has become too much of a commercial event had no impact on Ruth. Christmas was an important part of her life, and 1991 was no exception. As usual, they had the traditional Christmas Eve get-together with all the goodies. Ruth would spend many weeks every year preparing for the Christmas Eve celebration by baking cookies, shopping, and wrapping presents (many of which were made by her in craft classes).

"If I worked half as hard, it would probably kill me!" Tiny wrote. "By the time Christmas is over, I'm exhausted, just from watching her. Ruth is, if you haven't guessed by now, an amazing lady, and if I never received another Christmas present in my life, I would be more than satisfied."

Obviously, Ruth was Tiny's present for all seasons! To express his thoughts about her during the holiday season, Tiny wrote the following poem:

Me and Mrs. Santa Claus

I know what Mrs. Claus must ask,
    About this time each year.
When the bearded one begins his task,
    Of spreading Christmas cheer.

She wonders when this chubby gent,
    With all his magic powers,
Will lose the urge to go hell-bent,
    All throughout this land of ours.

When will he trade those bright red clothes?
    For a lazy man's attire,
Turn off the light in Rudolph's nose,
    And just sit by the fire.

How do I know all this? Because,
    I have undying proof.
There is a lady Santa Claus,
    That lives beneath my roof.

Like old Saint Nick, her Ho, Ho, Ho,
    Is such a welcome sound.
The grandest lady that I know,
    So nice to be around.

She does not drive a reindeer sleigh,
    She has no beard of white.
But, this female Santa has a way,
    Of making things just right.

Always in a festive mood,
    My Santa never wavers.
Making presents for her brood,
    For friends, and even neighbors.

Her nose is to the old grindstone,
> She starts in mid-September.
Works her fingers to the bone,
> No rest until December.

Yes, me and Mrs. Santa Claus,
> Both have the same request.
When will our busy Santas pause?
> And take time out to rest?

It's time to form a different team,
> Let others do their bit.
Oh yes, I know it's just a dream,
> These guys will never quit!

Written by D. V. Gillum

January 1, 1992 Tiny resolved to get busy and get himself in shape for the big event coming up in February. He was fearful of the scales, certain that the goodies consumed during the holidays would show up right there on the dial. The weight gain wouldn't make getting in shape any easier but Tiny knew what he had to do. He kept telling himself getting prepared for the camp would be no hill for a climber like himself! His main problem was having no one to work out with. Dave was working, and with the short daylight hours that time of year, there was hardly time to accomplish anything after his work day was over. Tiny began a regimen of daily flexibility exercises and running 30 and 40-yard sprints. Soon he was a sack of aching bones, but as time passed, so did the soreness. He had no one to play catch with, so he improvised. The school where Ruth attended craft class was formerly a junior high school with handball courts that were seldom used. By throwing the ball against the wall and catching the ball on the return, Tiny solved two problems: first, he worked out his throwing arm. Secondly, he practiced fielding ground balls. He visited local batting cages for hitting practice, concerned whether he would be able to follow the ball out of the pitching machine. This proved to be no problem for Tiny, but he still worried if the same would be true when he faced live pitching.

On the afternoon of January 31, Tiny picked Norv up at the airport. Norv was raring to go. Cath and Ruth would fly to Florida later. At 5:36 a.m. the next day Tiny and Norv pointed the Toyota Camry towards I-22 (Garden Grove Freeway) heading east on the first leg of their 2,700 mile journey. Traffic, heavier than expected, began to thin out by the time they were through Riverside. From then on the traffic was clear sailing. They reached Lordsburg, New Mexico the 1st day; about one fourth of their journey. Being a train buff, Norv kept his eye out for trains. Until they were out of California he had little luck, but as they neared Lordsburg and the main east-west Santa Fe thoroughfare, he raced up a score of about 10. That night was spent at a Best Western motel near the tracks where they heard about six more trains rumbling through town during the night. This was truly frosting on the cake for an avid train lover like Norv!

Next morning, expecting to get an early start, they were greeted by rain! Included in the room rent was a free breakfast at the restaurant next door, so Tiny and Norv decided to delay departure in hopes the rain might let up while they were eating. Big mistake! Everyone in the motel apparently had the same idea…and the café was short on waitresses. Served at long last, to get the "free" breakfast, they learned required a voucher from the motel, which they did not know about. They ended up paying for breakfast and losing at least 2 valuable hours of travel time. But, Norv did get to see a long east bound train; worth the wait, he would tell you. Seeing a train that early in the morning made them believe Norv would have another banner day of train watching. What they didn't know was that from Lordsburg the Santa Fe lines run northeast, while the highway paralleled the then unused Southern Pacific tracks. Knowing nothing about that, Norv had a good day scanning the horizon though. To top matters off, Tiny discovered later he had left his glasses in the café. No problem! He had spares!

The rains were steady, if the trains were not. Traffic was light though. They managed to reel off another 755 miles, stopping for the night in Seguin, Texas (about 25 miles from San Antonio). After a good breakfast in Seguin, they began the third leg of the journey still in steady rain. By the time they reached Houston, the steady rain had become a downpour of major proportions. Hitting Houston in such rain would have been bad enough, but the heavy traffic compounded the problem. Furthermore, those Texas "good old boys" didn't take too kindly to California license plates—if one can judge their attitude by the lack of courtesy they displayed Tiny while driving! Or, were they really that stupid? Most carry shotguns or rifles (or both) in racks behind the seat of their pickups, so Tiny and Norv didn't want to argue. Thankful to escape Houston with their lives, they continued east.

A few miles later they had come almost 900 miles across the state of Texas without so much as a spot of dry pavement. They began to feel better, hoping to see some of the land they were driving across. Driving through Lake Charles, Lafayette, Baton Rouge, and the "Big Easy" (New Orleans) was beautiful to say the least. Crossing Lake Pontchartrain fascinated both Tiny and Norv. Norv was really impressed by the size of this enormous body of water, and all the work that went into building the many bridges and highways in the area. They crossed at the narrowest point of the lake. Tiny wondered how much more thrilled Norv would have been had they taken the 26-mile bridge! From New Orleans they continued through Mobile, Alabama; Pensacola, Florida (Pepsi Cola according to Harv Langham); and, Clearview, Florida. Three driving days had put them within 400 miles of their destination.

At Clearview, Tiny and Norv found "free" breakfast meant just that at a Holiday Inn. A buffet, loaded with eggs cooked to taste, bacon, sausage, biscuits, gravy, fruit, pastries, cereals, and, naturally, "grits"! Tiny tried to talk Norv into trying the grits, but his Yankee breeding simply could not bend that far. The last leg of their trip without rain and with very light traffic put them at Dan and Beulah's at 2:15 p.m., 2.5 hours before Ruth and Cath were due to arrive. Since their ladies did not expect them to beat them there, they did not go to the airport; instead, they let Dan and Beulah go while they hid out at the house to surprise them!

Having left the rains at the Texas-Louisiana border, Tiny was shocked to find it raining in Daytona Beach the next morning. With 4 days before he would head south to West Palm Beach, Tiny began to think that old Murphy had struck again and that his fantasy camp adventure might be in jeopardy. Tornado warnings were issued for the area that day, causing Tiny to experience even more anxiety, not only because of his anticipated baseball camp. Tornadoes, to Tiny, were very frightening and the most difficult of nature's ways of getting our attention. As if the rain and threat of tornadoes was not enough, Tiny found a crack in his windshield above the wipers that extended all the way across.

Dan and Beulah McClellan had a nice home surrounded by big oaks and magnolias with abundant walking lanes throughout. This allowed Tiny to get back to his routine after spending 4 days behind the wheel of an automobile. The McClellans were a very devoted couple, and very nice people to be around. In addition to a heart condition, Dan had kidney problems that required him to have dialysis 3 times a week. Even so, they both remained very upbeat, jovial, and active.

In spite of all Tiny's worries, by 9 a.m. February 9 he was driving in sunny weather on his way to Baseball Heaven. Driving leisurely along Florida's east coast, Tiny enjoyed lightly wooded areas, small truck farms, citrus groves, beaches, and fishing villages. He arrived at the West Palm Beach Hilton, the official team headquarters for Baseball Heaven, at about 12:30 p.m. For once, old Murphy was busy with others. By 2 p.m., Tiny had a room assignment (some had to wait until after 6 p.m.). Tiny's roomie, Aaron Bor, was a 55-year-old attorney from Boston, Massachusetts. He was more apprehensive than Tiny! He thought himself too old for this "kid's game" until Tiny told him he was almost 67!

About 3 p.m., they took Tiny and Aaron a short distance to the Braves Minor League Complex where the camp would be conducted. There they were fitted with uniforms (which included a very nice "starter's jacket") and assigned lockers. They then met some of the ex-major leaguers who would be working with them during the camp. Tiny was quite thrilled to meet some of the players he had followed throughout their careers: Darrel Chaney, Doug Flynn, Johnny Sain, Lou Burdette, Bobby Wine, Glenn Hubbard, Rick Mahler, Tom Paciorek, Ralph Garr, and Bruce Dal Canton, among others. All of them were cooperative, friendly, and helpful. They gladly gave autographs free; none of the $10 to $50 fees children encounter at some baseball card shows!

Later at the hotel, Tiny and Aaron were invited to a welcome party at Clydesdales, a local night club. Tiny passed on that, letting the younger ones have that fun alone. Instead, Tiny had other problems on his mind. Just as he arrived at the hotel, a terrible noise under the hood of his car caught his attention. Knowing the coming week would be filled with much activity, he had no time for car trouble! He had arranged, through his insurance company, for the windshield to be replaced. Fortunately, the glass company would do the work at the hotel while he was playing baseball. This latest problem was another matter, however, and would have to be taken care of at a local dealer's establishment. Even so, the 1st day at Baseball Heaven had been eventful. Tiny was looking forward to the next morning when 104 "retreads" pranced on to the field to demonstrate their youthful prowess before a staff of old pros.

Up bright and early Monday morning found Aaron and Tiny, with another new friend, Dennis Clements from Fresno, California, in line for the breakfast buffet. They selected a table, and immediately were joined by none other than Johnny Sain, former Brave and New York Yankee great. This brought to Tiny's mind the phrase, "Spahn and Sain and pray for rain", referring to the Boston Brave's pitching rotation of 1948, when they won the National League pennant.

Johnny, in his middle 70's, delighted them with his agility and enthusiasm for the game. During a career spanning more than 50 years as player and coach, he compiled an outstanding personal record. He was a 20-game winner four times in 11 years; won 21 games and hit .347 in 1947; pitched nine complete games in 29 days in 1948; participated in four World Series as player or coach; and, produced 16 20-game winners in 14 years as a pitching coach. As unbelievable as all those accomplishments sound, Mister Sain had not yet been enshrined in the Baseball Hall of Fame! This certainly shows how much politics plays in the Hall of Fame selection process!

After breakfast, in a light rain, the men journeyed to the complex, and dressed for the day's activity. They then attended an information meeting where they were told, among other things, how the camp would be run. They also were advised that a Kangaroo Court would be conducted each morning at which players would be called to task and fined up to $5 for stupid things done the day before. The Fresno bulldog, Dennis Clements, was fined $5 that morning; at Clydesdales he let a barmaid wear and keep his hat at the welcoming party. Tiny had told Dennis to expect the fine the night before. Thus, he thought Tiny was the one who informed Bobby Wine of his actions. Therefore, Tiny was not surprised when he received a fine for carrying his autographed bat. He never could prove Dennis was the one, but Tiny did know misery loves company!

Next stop, the playing field—exercises were followed by being divided into several groups. Tiny joined the pitchers where they received tips from Johnny Sain, Lou Burdette, Rick Mahler, Ernie Johnson, and others. That afternoon they formed teams of 13 players per team, and played their evaluation games. The pros rated the camp participants on performance (just as Little League coaches did) in preparation for the draft scheduled that evening.

After the drafts were conducted that evening, the rosters were posted in the hotel lobby. At that point Tiny learned he was not the oldest in the camp. There were five others over 65. Three of those 5 were in their 70's! By 4 p.m. that 1st day, there were some dragging butts, including Tiny's'; but, he felt much better than he had expected.

Tiny was assigned to the Flynnstones, coached by Doug Flynn who had played 2nd base for the Cincinnati Reds, Philadelphia Phillies, and the Braves during his career. Average age of the team was 42. Tiny was the eldest of the lot! The pro coaches were very good with the players and let them play the position of their choice; but, make no mistake; they all expected the participants to play to WIN!

A rumor circulated that some hefty bets between the coaches were riding on the outcome. Beginning with Tuesday morning, they played a morning and afternoon game each day through Friday. On Saturday, the baseball part of this great week would end with a four inning game being played by each team against the pros. A banquet later that evening would cap off the week's festivities.

In addition to the regular scheduled games, each of the teams played a home and away game against fantasy teams from the New York Mets' training quarters at Port St. Lucie. Tiny's team, the Flynnstones, didn't fare too well the 1st day, losing both games. Although Tiny's pitching and defensive play was adequate, he went hitless in five times at bat. That was certainly not to his liking at all!

Tiny had decided early on not to push himself. Some of the fellows tried a little too hard and found themselves on the training room table with pulled muscles, strained ligaments, and worse. Two players (one a member of Tiny's team) suffered broken arms. There was one player who ended his fantasy the 1st day of play by pulling his hamstring tendon and biceps muscle in both legs! He was on his way back home before the action really got started. These mishaps only strengthened Tiny's resolve. With only a few days of camp, he was not about to forfeit any of his time there by doing something stupid; at least, not if he had any control over what happened.

On Wednesday morning, Tiny did something stupid alright but not on the baseball field. He decided to skip eggs for breakfast, and have biscuits and gravy instead. As he sat down to eat, he discovered his big mistake: He had covered his biscuits with grits, not gravy! He should have kept his big mouth shut! As soon as Tiny made the fact known to those at his table, he knew he had been had. Pat Jarvis, former Braves pitcher, heard Tiny's exclamation and, naturally, couldn't pass on that one. He later called Tiny up before the Kangaroo Court, fining him $2, saying it was shameful that "this old California boy" didn't know the difference between grits and gravy! Tiny wondered what the fine might have been had he admitted to being an old southern boy by birth!

Wednesday morning's game was a repeat of the day before. Tiny's team lost. He remained hitless but was not alone. Others were fanning out and popping up. Their fielding was no better than their hitting. That afternoon they played one of the Mets teams from Port St. Lucie. Although, they were a much younger bunch, the Flynnstones showed them! First, they jumped on their pitcher for five runs in the very first inning. The Flynnstones went on to win with a final score of 16-4. The trip back to the hotel that afternoon was a lot more fun. To finish the day, Tiny found the windshield in his car had been replaced during the day. He also was advised that the noise under the hood was only a frayed air conditioner belt. This, along with the team's first win, made Tiny one happy fellow!

That evening the camp participants attended a very interesting (at least, to Tiny) question and answer session. Any question was acceptable, so someone asked the panel of pros whether, in their opinion, Pete Rose should be banned from the Baseball Hall of Fame. Their response, a unanimous "no way", received thunderous applause from those present.

Thursday morning the Flynnstones won again defeating the "Scalpers" 6 to 4. In this game, Tiny played a couple innings at 2nd base before making his debut as a right fielder. His hitting streak, begun the day before, continued bringing his average up to a hefty (for him) .364. After lunch, the team made the journey to Port St. Lucie for a return encounter with the Mets. The drive of about 50 miles gave them a little longer rest between games than when they played two games back to back at home. Once more, they met a much younger team. Their pitcher was a big guy who could really "bring the ball". Again Tiny played right field and, to his surprise, made a fine running catch of a line drive hit his way. Entering the top of the sixth inning, the game was scoreless. Tiny had been to bat with no hits. In the sixth, as luck would have it, Tiny came to bat with two outs and runners at 2nd and 3rd. Their pitcher got ahead of Tiny by a count of two strikes and no balls. On his next pitch, Tiny singled through the hole between third and short, bringing in two runs to get a rally started! The Flynnstones went on to score two more runs, defeating the other team by a final score of 4-2. In addition to getting that key base hit, Tiny later singled, bringing his average up to .384! With this win, the team evened their record at three wins and three loses. The Flynnstones was beginning to remind Tiny of his 1983 Big League team…no stars, but a gang that wanted to play as a team, and win as a team.

Returning to the hotel that evening, Tiny found Ruth, which was a good thing. Knowing he was coming to the end of a fabulous dream, Tiny was starting to feel a little letdown coming on. He needed her support.

The Flynnstones ran their winning streak to five games, taking both on Friday: 11 to 7 and 3 to 2. These two wins allowed the team to finish camp with a record of five wins and three losses…good for a 3rd place finish in the final standings. Tiny was very well pleased with his personal record too getting seven hits in 20 times at bat for a .350 average. *Not too shabby*, Tiny thought, *for one my age who hadn't played in more years than I care to admit.*

That night Doug Flynn and his assistants treated the team to pizza and beer. As some time during the day's activities, Tiny had pulled a leg muscle, which began to ache while at the pizza place. He knew he had to resolve this problem quickly! There was no way Tiny was going to miss out on the "big game" Saturday. After the party, Tiny returned to his and Ruth's room. He immediately began ice pack applications. On Saturday, in better shape, but not out of the woods, he was first in line at the trainer's table. He applied hot liniment, after which he was treated to a great massage. *Good as new again*, or so he thought! On the lineup card Tiny was penciled in as the starting 2nd baseman, but he pulled the muscle again in the first inning having to come out of the game. Doug Flynn said he was sorry to see Tiny come out because he had scheduled him to pitch in the third inning. Well, that was all the motivation Tiny needed! He grabbed an ice bag and went to work on his leg. There was no way he was going to miss this opportunity to pitch to these stars of the past!

    The Flynnstones were scoreless through the top half of the third inning. In the bottom half, Tiny took the mound. He felt like a child whose dream had just come true! Playing against a team of ex-major leaguers was "the game of the week" for Tiny. The first batter he faced was Larry Jaster, a former Saint Louis Cardinal Pitcher. He popped up to the Flynnstones' shortstop! The next batter was Ralph Garr, a speedster and great hitter in his prime. Ralph had not been doing too well that day in the hitting department; so, he decided he would lay down a bunt and, lay one down he did! Neither Ralph nor Tiny could tell you how, but somehow, Tiny was on top of the bunt, and threw him out...throwing so hard Tiny thought his arm went with the ball. With two away, Glenn Hubbard, former 2nd baseman for the Oakland Athletics and later the Braves, hit a high pop fly to 2nd base which dropped untouched between the 2nd baseman and shortstop. With Glenn Hubbard on 2nd, the next player to come to bat was none other than one of Tiny's favorites, Lou Burdette, who was a pretty good hitter as well as an excellent pitcher. Lou hit a grounder to 3rd, and the 3rd baseman, in perfect style, threw him out. Tiny leaped with joy! If he had a sore muscle, he certainly didn't know it at that moment! Never in all Tiny's wildest dreams did he think at almost 67 years of age he'd face four ex-major league players without one of them hitting the ball out of the infield. Not even in a fantasy setting would Tiny have expected that great of a thrill!

Atlanta Braves Baseball Heaven "Fantasy Camp"
February 1992

At the banquet Saturday evening, Ralph Garr complimented Tiny, saying, "You're my man, you threw me out."

In response, at that point the old coach welled up inside, Tiny guessed, because he couldn't help smiling and saying, "You should have learned early in your career to never bunt back to the pitcher!" Tiny's reaction was all in good fun, which he and Ralph both knew.

Numerous trophies and awards were given out during the evening festivities—most valuable player, pitcher of the year, etc. Although Tiny didn't win any of those, he was given a trophy and selected to the "All Jim Lovell Team", something on the order of pro football's "All-Madden Team". Jim Lovell compiled his team each year. To qualify, one had to have been outstanding at "something" during the week. Tiny thought, *I earned mine by being fined more than any of the other players!* They made the absolute "most" of the evening, as Tiny tried not to think of this fabulous week being at an end.

Next morning Tiny and Ruth were back in the car headed west, back to reality. Baseball Heaven gave Tiny a package of unforgettable memories. He could not say enough in praise of the staff, their manner of conduct, and the total experience. The players he met there, from all professions, trades, and crafts…of all ages from about 30 up, and the way they melded together for a common thrill (just being "kids" again) was an unexpected bonus.

At Tallahassee Monday morning Tiny discovered his injured leg was quite swollen and bruised. The best he could do was soaking the leg, which he did. The next morning, confronted with problems of thunderstorms, Tiny and Ruth had difficulties getting back on the road. Ruth mislaid her glasses. Tiny got soaked loading their luggage. At Gulfport, Mississippi, they turned off the interstate to take more scenic Route 90, which meandered along the Gulf coast. A new camera, bought along the way, needed to be tried so they found a promising place where they could get some shots with the Gulf as a background. Leaving the car, they used some concrete steps leading down to a nice strip of smooth sand. Immediately they sank to their knees! Thinking they were in quicksand, Tiny lost his composure, as well as a shoe, trying to get out so he could help Ruth. In the meantime, with her usual cool, Ruth extricated herself…without the loss of a shoe or composure!

Later on Tuesday in New Orleans, Tiny and Ruth made their way with no little difficulty to the French Quarter where they expected to stay overnight. The price of hotel rooms very quickly changed their minds leading them to drive to the north side of town where prices were much more reasonable. The motel wouldn't have won any awards but the bed was good, which was what mattered most. From the motel, they booked a city tour and a river cruise for the next day. On their way to breakfast next morning, they heard more noises from under the hood. A service station attendant diagnosed the problem as the air conditioning compressor. He advised them they'd have no problem as long as they didn't use either the heat or air conditioner. That was later confirmed by telephone with a local Toyota dealer.

After breakfast, they boarded the bus for the city tour that wound in and around the French Quarter, Saint Louis Cathedral, the French Market, Preservation Hall, Dixieland Hall, and the Presbytère. Streets were one way and shared by cars, buses and pedestrians simultaneously. The tour was a mixture of new and old, churches, cemetery parks, and historical monuments interspersed with service stations, department stores, hotels, and, naturally, all the fast food joints! They also were shown the levees and canals that contained the Mississippi River and Lake Pontchartrain during times of flooding.

Much of New Orleans, 110 miles inland, is actually below sea level with the highest point only 30 feet above. At time of death, the affluent are interred in tombs above ground, while the less fortunate ones are buried underground. Underground burials pose problems because caskets float up during times of flooding. Therefore, those who are financially able choose the above ground method of interment.

Average annual rainfall, Tiny was told, was at that time over 59 inches in this city of approximately 500,000. That population was crowded into an area of less than 200 square miles (a density of approximately 2,500 people per square mile!) With Tiny and Ruth's city tour completed, they took the river cruise, which they could have skipped.

The river cruise was nothing more than the usual ships seen in any seaport, industrial complexes, and a Civil War battle site, where passengers were allowed 45 minutes ashore, then back to the dock. Their ship the Creole Queen might have been more appropriately named the Creole Trollop, according to what Tiny thought. The ship had nothing more to offer other than transportation, which could have been done in a dinghy.

Tiny and Ruth left New Orleans after the boat ride to spend that night in Baton Rouge, Louisiana. At San Antonio the next night, they checked into a Holiday Inn, but found the prices and accommodations far from comparable to what they had experienced elsewhere. A complaint to management resulted in a transfer to better.

Next stop, Las Cruces, New Mexico—and the first good Mexican dinner they'd had in a long, long time. After Las Cruces, the Gillum's goal was Sedona, Arizona via Lordsburg in hopes of retrieving Tiny's glasses left there, only to once more be disappointed. Their side trip to Sedona made up for the disappointment though. At that time Sedona was a quaint little town of some historical significance: mining, Indian wars, and notorious for brothels and Saturday night gunfights during the heyday of the Southern Pacific railroad construction. That night they set no alarm, intending to drive only as far as Williams the next day. Ruth, inveterate shopper that she was, had to make "one more" trip through the shops of Sedona before they left though!

U.S. Route 89 from Sedona at that time, according to Tiny, winded through some of the most magnificent scenery in Arizona, which has an abundance of beauty from deserts to mountains. They drove through Oak Creek Canyon along a winding road, awed by a winding creek and spectacular rock formations. The highway climbed to 7,000 feet, among majestic pine forests and patches of snow.

At Williams, Tiny and Ruth found another quaint little village that rolled up its sidewalks at dark, even on Saturday night. Arriving there in the afternoon, Ruth opted for a nap before dinner, expecting to get in some world class souvenir shopping afterwards only to discover that most of the shopkeepers in Williams had other ideas about how to spend their Saturday evenings. After a good night's rest (thanks in part to the shopkeepers of Williams) Tiny and Ruth set out the next day with Garden Grove in their sights.

Before leaving town, Tiny gassed up at an Exxon station. There the noise under the hood was finally stifled. The attendant found the source to be a loose air conditioning belt. He tightened the belt at no charge! Driving from Williams to Garden Grove was a "piece of cake". The total trip of 6,008 miles was made, Tiny was sure, with God sitting alongside with a hand on his shoulder. The minor problems they encountered could have been far worse. They were thankful to reach home safely.

***

CHAPTER 10

The Waning Years

If someone lived a sufficient amount of years after retirement, Tiny always thought the years from date of retirement to 80 years of age should be entitled "Retirement Years". Those years of survival past 80 years should be in an entirely different classification. Since at the time of Tiny's writing this chapter of his autobiography, he had already exceeded this 80-year limit, having reached 85 and having enjoyed retirement life for 26 plus years, he deemed the title of this chapter to be most appropriate. Therefore, no derogatory remarks are intended.

With all certainty, after the Florida trip Tiny was sure that he and Ruth would treasure the enjoyment of renewing relationships with relatives as well as the many friends they had not seen for some time. Being back in their "old stomping grounds" was very comforting to them! Tiny was sure Ruth was very eager to return to her craft class activities that she enjoyed. He was content with just to "keep on keeping on". The beginning of May, 1992 following the Florida trip was simply a continuance of the daily routine they left behind when they had begun the trip. On Monday, May 2, Ruth returned to her craft class; Tiny, of course, to his "do nothing" job. Although the time they had away from the routine on their Florida trip certainly had been a welcomed change, being able to return to what they enjoyed immensely was nice. For the next 5 years or so, Tiny and Ruth followed the same routine they had been content with for years. Ruth's priorities included frequent trips to visit

Cath and Norv in San Luis Obispo, her fervent desire to continue the craft classes that had been such an important part of her daily routine for so long, and the daily phone conversations with her "chit chat" friends and relatives. Tiny's passion was "sitting around" and practicing doing nothing. His "keep on keeping on" routine was more than agreeable with him. Then 1 day life changed!

As he did on each of Ruth's craft school attendance days, on that particular day Tiny drove to the school to give Ruth a ride home in another one of those rains that reminded Tiny so much of New Guinea (very unusual for California). She was not there! Tiny was told she had already departed. At first, Tiny thought they were just "putting him on", as they had been prone to do. However, this was not the case!

Immediately Tiny began the return journey home. About two blocks from their house, he found Ruth walking in that torrential downpour! All Tiny's pleading was to no avail. She very bluntly told Tiny that she was not going to get in his car because he had been too impatient to wait for her at school. She said, "You left me stranded there!"

Since Ruth was close enough to their house that Tiny could keep her in view, he continued on, keeping an eye on her as she continued her "stroll in the rain". When Tiny's dear lady arrived, Tiny said nothing to her, hoping that "silence would be the best treatment" for a while. However, when he tried to talk to her later, he received the same lack of cooperation as before. As time passed, Ruth's strange behavior continued, leading Tiny to make an attempt to convince her that perhaps he should make an appointment for her with their family physician for an overall assessment of her health, mental as well as physical. Wow! That was the wrong approach!

Immediately then Ruth informed Tiny that her health, both physical and mental, was as good, or better than his and that she was not in need of any doctor, or anyone else's opinion! When Tiny told her that he too would go through the same procedures that he had suggested she submit to affected her none whatsoever. Very bluntly she told Tiny that she was not going through any of that nonsense!

The Gillum's family physician had recently relocated to Nebraska, where he had accepted a position on the medical staff of one of the local hospitals in the city where he had planned to reside in his retirement. Tiny was already in the process of locating new medical services.

Previously Tiny and Ruth had made plans for her to visit her sister in San Luis Obispo, California for a period of 3 weeks or so. Tiny thought this would be the perfect time to locate new medical support and formulate the strategy he would need to assure that Ruth would receive the support that he thought she desperately needed.

Upon his return from driving Ruth to San Luis Obispo, Tiny contacted Hoag Memorial Presbyterian Hospital in Newport Beach, California. They provided Tiny with a list of physicians and surgeons who were members of their medical staff. From that list, Tiny chose what he determined to be an adequate replacement for Doctor Quinn. Tiny thought Thomas A. Goodheart, M.D., located in Huntington Beach, California, was very professional and friendly. Tiny soon discovered that he also was most knowledgeable in the field of medicine. Tiny could have never selected a more suitable medical professional for his lady.

Doctor Goodheart devised a plan that worked to perfection. He informed Ruth that he always recommended that his new patients submit to a full physical and mental evaluation to begin their relationship; thereby, providing him with a current medical summary. Surprisingly enough, Ruth agreed and they encountered no resistance whatsoever getting her to visit her new doctor. The results of this evaluation proved to be what Dr. Goodheart had suspected, the early stages of Alzheimer's disease. The good doctor then informed Tiny to not be too elated with the words "early stages", as the diagnosis almost always resulted in confinement to a nursing facility in the not too distant future. Tiny's immediate reaction to this was "This will be no hill for a climber like me! I will personally take care of my lady!" Oh! How wrong could one be!

During World War II, Tiny had served aboard the Unite States Navy Amphibious Landing Ship (LSM) #36 in the South Pacific Theatre of Operations. Their task encompassed the taking on, delivering to, and the landing of American Fighting Forces and their equipment on enemy controlled beaches under heavy enemy air attacks, as well as return fire from the enemy on shore positions. Their ship and crew participated in a total of 11 of these type landings, which, at times, involved scary situations. However, never once did Tiny recall feeling as helpless and frustrated as he did when he received the diagnosis of his precious lady's condition!

After almost 2 years of this 24 hour per day, 7 days per week task responsibility, Dr. Goodheart informed Tiny the time was past for Ruth to be admitted to a nursing facility. He told Tiny if he did not do so, there would be beautiful music being played around him that he would not be aware of! Although not fully convinced this was what Tiny should do, he "bit the proverbial bullet" and began his search for a suitable nursing facility. Tiny's first visit took him to a place that was very clean with a friendly attitude. However, there was one minus from Tiny's perspective: the facility bordered a street that was very heavy traffic laden, thereby creating a very relative high noise situation. Therefore, he more or less eliminated this facility.

The second place Tiny visited, "BINGO!!!"

As Tiny neared the receptionist's desk with his head hanging low, Tiny heard this lady say, "I know you!"

The receptionist behind the desk was a lady who was the mother of the most "gung ho" child baseball catcher Tiny had ever seen and coached in both Little League and later in high school! At that moment of recognition, Tiny immediately knew he would receive the "straight scoop" on the pros and cons of Extended Care Hospital of Westminster!

Extended Care Hospital, located in Westminster, California just off Hospital Circle, is situated a sufficient distance from Hospital Circle traffic that the noise factor from the traffic is almost nil. Extended Care was a 58-bed facility barely 2 miles from the Gillum home in Garden Grove, which truly was a blessing. Tiny was not at all surprised to find they had a waiting list. Immediately, Ruth became number 37 on that list!

Approximately 6 months prior, Tiny had discovered that a combined ship's reunion for LSM crew members from LSM 36 and LSM 299 had been started by one of the 299 crew members who was a resident of Charlotte, North Carolina and in the process of searching for former crew members of LSM 299. Mr. T. D. Burns, a radioman on the 299, was very dedicated and the most relentless individual Tiny thought he had ever had the pleasure of knowing in all his years on planet earth. This fine gentleman had spent an unknown amount of time, as well as dollars on an unending effort to locate fellow crew members of the LSM 299. During his search, he located a former officer aboard the LSM 36 almost next door to him in Charlotte. William Kenny, IV, final skipper of the 36 was that "next door" gentleman. Skipper Kenny "called the shots" during the final days leading up to the decommissioning of the "Grandest Lady of them all", who was a vital part in the defeat of an enemy hell-bent on the takeover of the greatest nation ever known to mankind.

Burns and Kenny worked together and took on the task of locating other crew members of both ships. This is how Tiny became aware of the reunion activity. The next reunion was scheduled for June 2001, which placed Tiny in somewhat of a bind, in that he was hoping he could have the transfer of Ruth to the nursing home completed long before the start of the reunion. This, of course, would depend entirely on how rapidly the extended care waiting list reduced in number.

In April, 2001 the Gillum's received a notice that an opening had become available. Tiny prayed and pondered about this tremendous decision that he needed to make. Finally, he turned down the opening! He just could not say yes at that time because he knew they would not lose their position on the list and he needed more time. Well, that time was very short in duration! Less than 1 month later they received notice of another opening! This time Tiny knew he had no choice other than to agree. May 30, 2001 was a date

Tiny never forgot! He had performed some heartbreaking tasks in his life; however, none could ever remotely approach the severity of this one! One of Tiny's greatest concerns was how Ruth would react when the time came for him to depart for home leaving her behind in an entirely different environment. All his worrying was for naught! When he kissed Ruth goodbye, her reactions were no different than what they had always been at home. Apparently, Ruth did not realize the difference in location whatsoever, as she blended in with her new surrounding very well.

Tiny departed for his reunion with his former Navy buddies in Omaha. Although he did enjoy his reunion with several of his shipmates he had not seen for many years, his mind was always on his lady at the Extended Care facility in Westminster. Upon his return to Garden Grove, Tiny immediately visited Extended Care to discover things could not have gone any better! When he asked Ruth how long he had been gone, she said, "You have been gone at least 2 hours."

Ruth's response reinforced Tiny's belief that God still performed miracles! This was a true blessing to know that not only was Ruth receiving outstanding care at Extended Care, she also was receiving the Lord's blessings. This brought to mind the often heard saying, "God works in mysterious ways!"

In addition to providing what proved to be the finest care one could have ever hoped to receive in any hospital, the care Ruth received at Extended Care exceeded any personal care Tiny had provided or could have provided at home. The dedication and care displayed by the staff at Extended Care was by far the best Tiny had seen in any hospital that he had been associated with. Ruth's care at Extended Care also was far superior to any care Tiny could have been able to give her. Although he did have reservations about not being with her during his reunion excitement, Tiny very much enjoyed seeing some of the former sailors he had spent so much time with on the 36. Other reunions followed, with the last one being in 2008. During his trip to attend the 2008 reunion, Tiny also made his last visit to see relatives who still lived in the Ashland area. That's for another chapter, which one of Tiny's surviving relatives will write about.

While not attending later reunions or visiting relatives back East, Tiny visited Ruth daily, sometimes walking the 2 miles from his home. During a conversation with his late Aunt Earl's granddaughter Pam Owens during a visit to Kentucky in 2003, Tiny spoke of how many individuals often asked him, "Why do you do it? Why are you so dedicated to visit Ruth daily when she doesn't even know who you are?"

"She may not know who I am, but I know who she is," was always his reply. This spoke deeply to Pam of the depth of Tiny's love and commitment to Ruth, setting an example of a "marriage made in Heaven", as Tiny's Aunt Earl would have described Tiny and Ruth's marriage.

Pictured above is Tiny with his wife Ruth in the later stages of her Alzheimer's disease. Photo taken Christmas season 2006

As the pattern had been with many other residents Tiny had seen at Extended Care, Ruth's condition continued to worsen. At 5:10 p.m., October 5, 2007 her suffering ended, as she peacefully entered Paradise. For those who might ask did Tiny feel angry, the answer is no. Grief and much pain, yes, but, he fully realized that her death at that time was God's will. He also was most confident that he and Ruth would be together once more when his Lord called him home.

The dedication Tiny saw at the extended care facility displayed to each resident (not just his lady) led Tiny to classify Extended Care Hospital of Westminster as "The Eighth Wonder of the World". As Tiny often did to better describe his feelings about matters that he deemed worthy, he wrote the following poem shortly after Ruth's arrival at Extended Care as a tribute to "The Eighth Wonder of the World".

Angels in Waiting

For weeks, my mind has worked overtime,
To analyze things I perceive.
At Extended Care where devotion is prime,
Where staff members truly believe.

They believe each resident has every right,
To dignified care and respect.
Therefore, remain present both day and night,
To maintain a calming effect!

There, forty plus residents including my wife,
Are completely dependent on others.
Alzheimer's patients from all walks of life,
Wives, husbands, fathers, and mothers.

When I see lovely people like these,
To me, there is no debating.
I most certainly never see Alzheimer's disease,
I only see "Angels in Waiting"!

Forty plus residents, craving much love,
All angels in my humble view.

The Waning Years

Angels in waiting to join God above,
In Heaven where life starts anew!

In Heaven, our angels will readily find,
A life that is never unfair.
No more confusion will enter their mind,
There will be no sorrow to bear!

No wheelchairs, no walkers, no bitter pills.
No IV insertions in veins.
Heaven is free from all earthly ills,
Not even the memory remains!

Breathing and eating no longer a chore,
Feeding tubes now will be history.
Recognition of others, normal once more,
Surroundings are never a mystery.

No more confinement behind big double doors.
No danger that anyone will fall.
Angels in waiting, both mine and yours,
Will have no problems at all!

To the fantastic staff at Extended Care,
Who pamper, console and protect.
On our angels' behalf, I firmly declare,
You have our utmost respect!

Written by D. V. Gillum

***

Editor's Note: As much as my cousin Duard Vinson Gillum, always known to me as "Tiny", impacted my life for the better, a few weeks ago after rereading the conclusion in his autobiography *Recollections of a Common Man* (Xlibris, 2011), I felt compelled by the Holy Spirit to carry out his last request made in his book. His conclusion* follows:

IN CONCLUSION

As I bring this narrative to a close, allow me to call attention to a fact that most of us know but …perhaps…overlook in our daily lives. When I was a youngster…before the days of television (and, with radio available to only the more affluent), families talked …about ancestors…about friends…about relatives…about neighbors…about God, and about life and death, and all the wondrous things between, that are in our lives. Today, we tend to overlook the value of those discussions, and the lessons to be learned thereby.

This book, in addition to being a chronicle of my life and times, is left to those who will succeed me, whether they be family or friends, or both. To them, I entrust the final chapter, hoping that someday, someone will take what is thus far advanced and carry it forward…that he, she, or they will chronicle events subsequent to these and of their lives and times…and in so doing, continue this as a book of Family Heritage. Otherwise, by the time my successors shall have reached this point in their lives, there may be no means to bridge the gap of intervening years…DVG

(*Retrieved from *Recollections of a Common Man*, p. 211)

CHAPTER 11

Just like an Uncle!
By Pamela K. Orgeron

"Your dad has always, and will continue to feel more like a brother to me than a cousin, and the word adoption never enters my mind. I love each of you as much, if not more than distant relatives I have not seen in many years, and certainly others I have never met."

The above quotation is excerpted from an email sent to me Tuesday, March 16, 2010 from my cousin Tiny. He and I were communicating then regarding the search that my father was doing back then to try to find out whether Dad had any biological siblings still alive. Unfortunately, despite all his efforts, Dad was unable to solve that mystery before his passing. Tiny understood Dad's desire to want to know the truth about his family of origin; yet Tiny loved Dad no less because he was adopted. Tiny and Dad always spoke of how they felt more like brothers to each other than cousins. Given their close relationship, I think the fact that especially in Tiny's later years he seemed more like an uncle, or even a "grandfather figure" than a cousin to me would make sense. No doubt, Tiny's being a brother in Christ also gave much more depth to our relationship.

Being about 11 years older than Dad and since my paternal adopted grandparents received him within a few days of his birth, Tiny knew Dad all his life. I also think the fact that my paternal grandparents, Tiny's Uncle Harry and Aunt Earl, cared so much for Tiny in his younger years also contributed to the strong bond he had with our family. Not to mention how Tiny's mother, my Great Aunt Ida, was a regular guest at our home during the holidays after Tiny and his brothers moved away from Ashland. My family also visited Aunt Ida frequently in between special occasions, sometimes taking her shopping whenever we took her sister, my Mama Owens.

My first recollections of hearing about Tiny were sitting around the dinner table each Thanksgiving and Christmas listening to the stories about Aunt Ida's sons in California and her one son in Baltimore. No doubt, Tiny remembered me as a baby and during my younger years from the rare occasions that he was able to visit relatives in Ashland. Dad always made a point to see Tiny whenever he was in town. They also talked on the telephone periodically.

The earliest memories I have of seeing Tiny in person go back to when I was in early grade school. To be honest, I didn't always feel a close bond with Tiny and his family. Only remembering stories about Tiny and his family from my early years and then to have them show up "out of the blue" as extended family live and in person, they were like strangers to me. Furthermore, at that point in my life I didn't warm up too well with any man (stemmed back to the sexual abuse in my past). And I definitely didn't like boys, which included Tiny's son Dave!

Dave was from my birthday, April 28 to his birthday, August 7 younger than me. I remembered warming up to Ruth then but not the males in the Gillum family. What I couldn't stand about Dave was how he always picked on (teased) me back then. I remember complaining to Mom, Ruth, Mama Owens, and other female relatives present then about how I didn't like Dave because "He picks on me too much."

In response to my concern, the women only laughed at me, as Ruth said, "That just means he likes you."

Mom and Mama Owens all agreed with Ruth, saying, "When boys pick on girls, that just means they like them."

In late elementary school I remember Dad and Mom discussing how Dad was approaching a certain number of years of employment where he would get a 13 weeks' vacation. Dad wanted to go see Tiny in California and take us children to Disneyland. He would take 10 weeks of the 13 weeks' vacation during the summer which would enable us to drive to and from California sightseeing along the way. Mom really didn't want to make the trip then because her father was in a nursing home at that time; but she went along for Dad's sake. I didn't want to go either. I remember begging Dad and Mom to let me stay with Mama Owens, who would be housesitting for us while we were gone.

Looking back I'm glad my parents forced me to go on the trip even though I didn't remember the Gillum family from their visits to our home in previous years. Not remembering much about Tiny and his family other than the fact that he was Aunt Ida's son, I was slow to warm up to Tiny when we arrived at the family's home that summer in 1972. However, before our visit ended, I grew to love the entire Gillum family.

California Trip Photos—Summer 1972

L to R: Patty Owens, Ruth Gillum, Pam Owens, Tiny Gillum

Top L to R: Tiny's Brother Cliff with grandchildren and wife Norma
Left: Cliff with his daughter Mimi
Bottom: At Disneyland-Tiny is driving, Passenger is Dave. Backseat: Ruth, Pam, Patty. Patrick Owens is hanging on.

Just like an Uncle!

L to R: Dave; Pam waving, and Patty behind her; Tiny; Marvin; and Ruth

While visiting the Gillum family summer 1972 I vaguely remember Tiny telling Dad that we came out just in time because his employer was talking about transferring him to Ohio. My next memories of Tiny and his family were after they moved to Ohio and had decided to return to California. I remember how sad Aunt Ida, Mama Owens, and everyone else in the family, including me, was about them returning to California.

Two memorable in-person visits I had with Tiny as an adult were in 2003 and 2008 when he was staying with Mom and Dad during these trips east to visit relatives in Kentucky and to attend his annual reunion with his Navy buddies. By 2003 I was living in Morehead, KY attending graduate school but when Mom called me to tell me that Tiny and Dave were coming in and that Tiny said he wanted to see me, I was quick to take a break from my studies to be able to spend time with Tiny and Dave. On one particular day during their visit while Dad and Tiny ran around together visiting old haunts and other relatives whom Dave and I did not know as well, I took Dave to Morehead to visit my apartment and to see the local sights there.

Tiny's Trip "Home"—2003

Pam Owens and Dave Gillum
Photo taken at Morehead State University, Morehead, KY

First Cousins Marvin Owens, Tiny Gillum, and Elvin Adkins
(Photo taken in Morehead, KY)

L to R: Dave Gillum, Pam Owens, Tiny Gillum

L to R: Missy, Sharon, and Bob Layman with Bob's First Cousins Marvin Owens and Tiny Gillum

L to R: Ruth and Tiny Gillum with unknown person at nursing home. Tiny mailed me a copy of this photo along with the photos he took in Kentucky in 2003. I would be amiss to not include the photo in the "final" chapter of Tiny's life story.

Tiny's visit east in 2008 would be his last trip "home" to his roots. During that time Dad put together a family reunion at one of the local restaurants inviting all the cousins along with their families. Tiny's cousins who attended included: Aunt Flaura's sons, Bill and Bob Layman (and his wife Sharon); Aunt Phoebe and Uncle Audie's children, Jan Short, Nagatha Kendrick (husband Bill), along with members of their family. Of course, Donna and Pete O'Connor and my family also were present for the reunion. That visit ending was difficult because we knew we'd never see Tiny again, at least here on earth. I thank God for the photos and memories I have of Tiny at that time.

Tiny Says "Goodbye" to "Home"—2008

Family Reunion at Longhorn Steakhouse, Ashland, KY
Patty, Pam, and Marvin Owens with Tiny Gillum
(Tiny insisted we stand under the American Flag.)

L to R: Donna & Pete O'Connor, Tiny Gillum

L to R, Front Table: Pam Owens, Pete and Donna O'Connor. L to R, Back Table: Bob and Sharon Layman, Name Unknown; Ron Adams (Standing), Marvin Owens. Tiny was sitting between Ron and Marvin. Photo taken by Patty Owens

L to R: Sharon and Bob Layman, Tiny Gillum

L to R: Nagatha Adams Kendrick, Pete and Donna O'Connor

L to R: Brothers Bob & Bill Layman with Cousins Tiny Gillum, Ron Adams, & Marvin Owens

**Photo taken at 1022 Berkshire Lane, Russell, KY
L to R: Patty & Marvin Owens, Tiny Gillum
Donna & Pete O'Connor**

Tiny's and my bond continued to grow as we communicated a lot over the telephone those last couple of years or so before he died. I remember a year or so before Tiny's death he talked to me a lot about how he could already hear the Heavenly choir singing different hymns and that he didn't have long left on earth. He said I was the only one with whom he shared that because he said if he told anyone else, they'd think he was crazy. Tiny wasn't crazy; and I knew that; he was sensitive to how God was working in his life.

In early 2010 my fiancé Milton J. Orgeron and I were planning a June wedding in Morehead, KY that year. When I learned that my father would be unable to attend to give me away and expressed the situation to Tiny, in an email dated April 30, 2010, he wrote

> Pam, I sure am sorry that your dad will miss out on your wedding...If I was not using all my time sitting in doctor offices, I would grab a handful of Amtrak and be there, and walk you or tote you down the aisle if you so desired...Your cuz.

That email was so sweet that I cried when I received the message! Later Milton and I postponed our June wedding for us to be married during the Christmas season, my favorite time of the year.

Though Tiny and I never saw each other again in person after 2008, Milton was blessed to meet Tiny during the fall of 2010 before we would be married in December. I'll let Milton share his memories of that time below:

Tiny Gillum is one of the many significant people in Pam's life that I wish I had met years ago and had much more time to get to know better. Tiny and Marvin were certainly brothers in the same wonderful spirit as much as though they had been biological siblings. He was always a pleasure to talk with over the phone, and a great encouragement then and in our email correspondence.

I finally got to meet Tiny in person only less than a year before he passed away, through a weeklong business trip that took me to Pomona, CA, about 30 miles from his home in Garden Grove, CA. We arranged for me to meet Tiny and his son and other relatives Wednesday night for dinner.

Of course, I got lost for a while on the way, driving without a GPS with only printed directions. But after a few wrong turns I did find Tiny and crew about a half-hour late. Tiny and his family were gracious hosts and it was a very enjoyable dinner and meeting.

After dinner, we drove to Tiny's home where he and I and his son Dave talked for a few hours. The evening was all too short nevertheless, and I had to get back to the hotel or face Los Angeles area morning rush hour traffic and likely be late for the next morning's work sessions.

That meeting was to be the one and only time I met Tiny in this life, and it was undoubtedly God's timing for my business trip to be when and where it was. I miss the wonderful person I met then, and look forward to seeing him and many others again in God's time. Now back to Pam's part of the story.

On November 23, 2010 I emailed Tiny an informal invitation to Milton's and my wedding scheduled December 10 that year. Tiny replied, "Pam-Congratulations! Wish I could be there, but impossible. My very best to both of you. By the way, I think you have a real W-I-N-N-E-R!!!! .... Your Cuz" That was another one of Tiny's tear-jerking messages to me!

I still have the email dated December 20, 2010 sent to me from Tiny where he broke the news to me that he had cancer. That message crushed me.

Sunday, February 27, 2011 I emailed Tiny asking how he was doing and how his treatment was going. He replied back the same day with the following message (originally in ALL CAPS with a few grammatical errors, which I have edited),

> Pam – As for my treatment, I began a series of shots a couple weeks ago that is supposed to be very promising for either curing or stopping the cancer, I am not sure which. My take on this whole thing is, if I did not do anything, it would be ok with me. I am now 5 months short of age 86 and, I feel very fortunate to have lived this long. God has been good to me. He brought me through a bout with double pneumonia and measles (at the same time) when I was about 6 weeks old. He saw me through the Great Depression days. He saw me through World War II where I participated in 11 invasions serving aboard a naval landing ship that ferried invading troops to the beaches, and unloaded those troops under enemy fire, and I only received one injury, and that was not in action. I cut my right index finger while cutting out a portion of a "zero" insignia on a Japanese Zero Fighter Plane. God has treated me great and I have no complaints. The day he says "come on", I will have no problem with being with Ruth again!

I do what the doctors say because this pleases the kids. They all treat me like a king (this includes Ruth's three that were barely teenagers when we were married) and, they all will and do tell everyone that asks that I am their dad. Pam, I had a good life and, I have no complaints. As for my book, it is now completed by the publishers and is available for sale. I have had requests for about 20 copies from relatives and friends and, I will do my best to comply with each request. You and Patrick will be added to that list.

    Your Cuz

As promised after the above email, Tiny mailed us a copy of his autobiography *Recollections of a Common Man* (Xlibris, 2011) officially published in early 2011. We received our copy Saturday, May 14, 2011.

Tiny and I continued to communicate via phone or email right up until his death July 3, 2011, His last message to me was sent about 2 weeks before his passing. Knowing Tiny's death was imminent my last "goodbye" message to him was sent the day before he died, which I requested Dave read to him knowing he probably couldn't respond. I still grieve his loss, but look forward to our Heavenly reunion.

***

Both Gone, But Not Forgotten!

I love and miss them both!
My Father Marvin Owens & Cousin D. V. "Tiny" Gillum
(This is the last photo I made of just them two together on their last visit with each other.)

***

Appendix

A Tribute to Mam-Maw Keaton

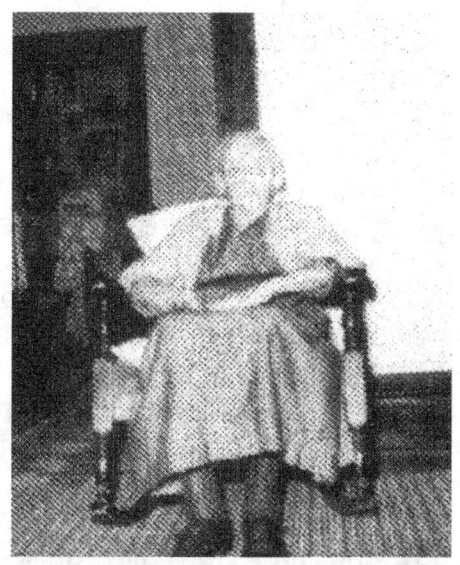

Mary Melissa Keaton Smith sitting in her rocker that no one else dared sit in.

Who impacted Tiny's life the most? He would tell anyone his Mam-Maw Keaton. Additionally, he felt including a tribute of worthy proportion should be included of her along with his story. To not do so, Tiny felt his own story would be incomplete and insincere.

Born January 7, 1874, at Smith's Creek, Kentucky, Mary Melissa Keaton, was "Mam-Maw" to Tiny. Mam-Maw's education, though informal and not from "book larnin'" as she would have said, was from the experience of life by word of mouth and the deeds of heart, hand, and soul. She was a product of the people of her time, strong willed and purposeful...molded by the hand of fate and tempered by the hand of God.

Mam-Maw's life was not easy. In fact, what she experienced in life would have crushed most people who were born at a later time and in another place. Children of Mam-Maw's time were expected to work in the fields and shoulder their share of the family burden. School, if any, was much less important than the need for family sustenance and was relegated to a secondary position in all but the most affluent families of that region.

In October of 1955, word came to Tiny that Mam-Maw was gravely ill and might not survive the remainder of that year. Then no more than 2 months short of her 82nd birthday, visiting her in life rather than viewing her in death was vital to Tiny. Taking a week of his accrued vacation time, Tiny flew to Huntington, which was the nearest commercial airport to Ashland. Due to a misunderstanding, Tiny's Aunt Phoebe and Uncle Audie thought Tiny would be arriving in Charleston, 45 miles to the east. With no one at the airport to meet him, Tiny took an airport shuttle bus and ended up going directly to Mam-Maw before seeing any other family members, which turned out to be for the best. She seemed elated to think Tiny had come from so far away (to her, California was still a distant and untamed land; the Far West of her childhood) and had not "dilly dallied" with others before coming to her bedside. Knowing her end was near, Tiny was grateful to have had those last few days with her. When he flew home, Tiny carried a flood of memories of this woman whom he referred to as the "Grandest Lady" of them all. She died December 14, 1955 at the age of 81 years, 11 months, and 6 days. This chapter will include Tiny's memories of his "Mam-Maw".

In 1895 Mary Melissa Keaton married Augustus (Allie) Smith. Twin sons were born of that union a year later but both died in infancy. Tiny's mother, Ida May Smith, was born to them April 26, 1897, followed by a brother Thurman and four sisters (Ethyl, Flaura, Phoebe, and Earl). In 1927, for reasons unknown to Tiny, she and the man Tiny knew as

A Tribute to Mam-Maw Keaton

Pap-Paw parted company. At that time, Mam-Maw settled in the Ashland area.

A tiny woman, Mam-Maw wore her hair rolled in buns. When not rolled, as when she washed or patiently brushed it, her hair draped to the floor. She had no faith in doctors and scorned dentists. She relied entirely on home remedies, no doubt handed down from generations before. If her remedy failed to cure a toothache, she pulled the tooth...using ordinary wire pliers! For chest colds, she applied mustard plasters. Constipation called for large doses of castor oil and Epsom salts. Her fundamental cure-all was a mixture of camphor and whiskey. The word "vitamin" was unknown to her. Other than for "medicinal purposes", she never used alcohol.

Mam-Maw did favor a dip of snuff now and then, and her clay pipe was a constant companion. Her tobacco (the only brand she was ever known to smoke) was "Strater's Natural Leaf"...a blend, Tiny suspected, of tobacco, pine pitch, and dynamite! Tiny lit her pipe once...and only once...and thought by doing so that he had blown a hole in the back of his head! The mixture never bothered her though. She smoked her pipe all day, every day, as long as she lived.

To Tiny, Mam-Maw was a combination of Florence Nightingale (because of her unique medical expertise) and Theodore Roosevelt (who, like Mam-Maw, spoke softly, but carried a big stick). She was a hearty soul who ate corn bread and green beans for breakfast, along with the salt pork that she always used for seasoning. Her favorite beans were what she called "leather britches". Using a regular sewing needle, she patiently strung the beans on threads stretched across the room. Row upon row, the beans hung near the ceiling for whatever number of days required for drying. When dried, the beans looked and felt like coarse leather britches, hence the name. The beans did not look too appetizing, but after cooking all day, they were as tender as fresh green peas and far tastier.

Bakery bread was beneath Mam-Maw's scorn. When speaking of light bread (so called in the south, referring to bakery white bread), she would say, "It's alright for the kids to roll up in a little ball and play with, but it ain't fit to eat."

A private person, Mam-Maw lived by her rules and never meddled in the affairs of others, unless called upon to "speak her mind". On such occasions, one could expect to hear her perspective exactly as she saw the matter; she never minced her words. Whether her thoughts were complimentary or otherwise, she voiced her honest opinion. Thus, if one wanted only good news or agreement, Mam-Maw wasn't the one to consult. Straightforward, as she was, Mam-Maw would not tolerate pampering or soliciting. For example, Tiny recalled a day when a fruit peddler stopped his Model-T Ford in the back alley, asking Mam-Mam, "Would you like to buy some apples?"

"No, thanks," she said simply puffing on her pipe and rocking.

Thinking to generate her interest, the man told Mam-Maw how cheaply he was selling his apples. Again, she declined. Persisting, he said to her, "They are awful good eating apples."

"If they are so good, you eat 'em," she said. That ended the conversation.

Mam-Maw had a unique version of the English language with expressions that were clearly her own. When threatening Tiny or one of the other children with punishment, she would say, "Stop it, or I'll whip you lengthwise, just like whipping a yeller dog."

On occasion, Mam-Maw also was known for voicing an unsolicited opinion, but always about someone or something other than those immediately present. Tiny recalled one such occasion: One afternoon while sitting and rocking, she spied a young lady across the street wearing very short shorts. To no one in particular, Mam-Maw snorted, "I want you to look at that 'thang'! You can see plumb up to her forks!"

On a later visit to Ashland, Aunt Phoebe gave Tiny Mam-Maw's old rocking chair...the one in which no one else dared to sit. Tiny had the chair refinished and gave the chair a place of honor in his living room to constantly remind him of this remarkable lady. Tiny once wrote a poem describing Mam-Maw, whom he saw as a one of a kind woman who remained in his memory as long as he lived. Tiny's poem will conclude the tribute to "Mam-Maw":

**Mother
Mary Melissa
Smith
Jan.7, 1874-
Dec. 14, 1955
IN HEAVEN THERE'S
ONE ANGEL MORE**

My Mam-Maw

The other day these thoughts of mine,
    Went back to early scenes,
Back to the days when things were fine,
    Without our modern means.

I remember my dear Mam-Maw well,
    When I was just a kid,
I marveled at this Southern Belle,
    And all the things she did.

If Mam-Maw were alive today,
    How would she handle things?
What would this grand old lady say,
    About what progress brings?

The computer age would blow her mind,
    My memory still lingers,
Come counting time, she was inclined,
    To use her toes and fingers.

How would she feel about fast food,
    That is microwaved to suit?
She cooked with wood for all our brood,
    And built the fire to boot.

Soap that squirts, soap on a rope,
    Are popular kinds we buy.
Mam-Maw always made her soap,
    With bacon grease and lye!

Electric blankets some have said,
    Are the warmest things for naps.
She covered up her feather bed,
    With a quilt she made from scraps.

Space Shuttle flights that we all hail,
    To her would be no boon.
No way would she believe the tale,
    We landed on the moon.

To those who use cocaine and "grass",
    She would truly hate your type.
But she liked tea with sassafras,
    And, tobacco for her pipe.

Some modern folks who read my rhyme,
    Will say I'm just a fretter.
But, if we regressed to Mam-Maw's time,
    Our world would be much better!

***

About the Editor

Pam Orgeron

Pamela K. Orgeron, M.A., Ed.S., BCCC, ACLC, formerly Pamela K. Owens (1960-) was born in Ashland, KY. In 1986 she received a B.A. degree in Journalism-Public Relations from Marshall University, Huntington, WV. Also in 1986 Ms. Owens moved to Nashville, TN where she spent over 8 years employed with the Jean and Alexander Heard Library, Vanderbilt University. Before moving back to Kentucky in 2000, she also worked for Harris Publishing and Thomas Nelson Publishers. Ms. Owens received both an M.A. (2003) and an Ed.S. (2009) degree in Adult & Higher Education, Counseling Specialization from Morehead State University, Morehead, KY. Ms. Owens moved back to Nashville in 2009. Since then she has received an Advanced Diploma in Biblical Counseling from Light University and became a Board Certified Christian Counselor and a Board Certified Advanced Christian Life Coach. In 2010 she married Milton J. Orgeron. She and Milton are General Partners in *ABC's* Ministries, and are members of The Donelson Fellowship Freewill Baptist Church, Nashville, TN. Mrs. Orgeron also is a certified writer with the Institute of Children's Literature, West Redding, Connecticut.

> **Pamela K. Orgeron, M.A., Ed.S., BCCC, ACLC**
> Christian Author, Counselor, & Life Coach
> General Partner, *ABC's* Ministries
> For more information about *ABC's* Ministries:
> Visit our Website:
> https://abcsministries.wordpress.com/

About the Editor

Books by Pam Orgeron:

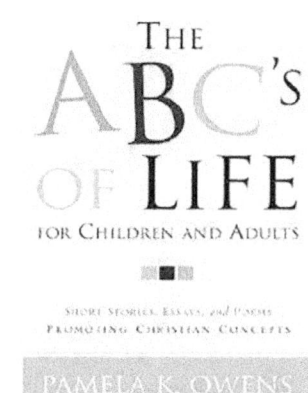

ISBN PB 1-594670-08-0
ISBN HB 1-594670-09-I

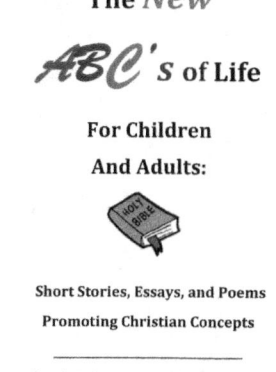

ISBN PB 978-0-692-63950-4
ISBN HB 987-0-692-70398-4

ISBN PB 978-0-9979565-0-4
ISBN 978-0-9979565-2-8 (e book)
ISBN HB 978-0-9979565-1-1

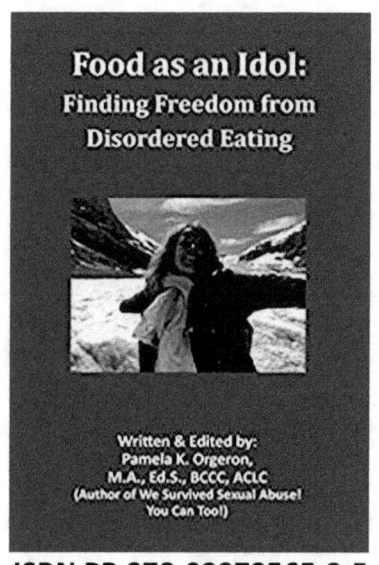

ISBN PB 978-09979565-3-5

www.ingramcontent.com/pod-product-compliance
Lightning Source LLC
Chambersburg PA
CBHW070540010526
44118CB00012B/1183